IT GIRL

ALSO BY MARISA MELTZER

Glossy

This Is Big

Girl Power

How Sassy *Changed My Life* (coauthor)

IT GIRL

THE LIFE AND LEGACY OF JANE BIRKIN

Marisa Meltzer

ATRIA BOOKS
New York Amsterdam/Antwerp London
Toronto Sydney/Melbourne New Delhi

ATRIA BOOKS

An Imprint of Simon & Schuster, LLC
1230 Avenue of the Americas
New York, NY 10020

First Atria Books hardcover edition October 2025

ATRIA BOOKS and colophon are trademarks of Simon & Schuster, LLC

Interior design by Davina Mock-Maniscalco

Manufactured in the United States of America

3 5 7 9 10 8 6 4

Library of Congress Control Number: 2025940403

ISBN 978-1-6680-6028-5
ISBN 978-1-6680-6030-8 (ebook)

CHILTERN: You prefer to be natural?

CHEVELY: Sometimes. But it is such a very difficult pose to give up.

Oscar Wilde, *An Ideal Husband*

CONTENTS

IT GIRL

INTRODUCTION

Jane Birkin's very own, original Birkin bag looks like she dug it out of a shipwreck. In the documentary *Jane B. par Agnès V.*, by the legendary French New Wave director Agnès Varda, we watch the film for about twenty minutes to see its reveal. The camera is focused on the black leather holdall with its fraying handles and rich, mottled patina across the leather, especially on the high-traffic areas.

"Now, let the cat out of the bag," instructs Varda off-camera, filming the bag's big moment. "Yes, no problem," says Birkin, who dutifully dumps out its contents. Out tumble multiple notebooks, a Swiss Army knife, newspaper clippings, Maybelline Great Lash mascara, pencils, cash, cigarettes, a Dostoyevsky novel, Scotch tape: an everywoman's survival kit. It was custom-designed for her in the 1980s to be utilitarian, to fit everything she needed to be out and about with a baby in tow.

Initially all we can see of Birkin the woman is a torso clad in a tweed blazer and her legs in faded blue jeans. It's only after the bag is captured on film that Varda shows us the face of its illustrious namesake. Jane Birkin is beautiful, but even more than that, she is memorable. Her lips are full and pouty. There's a gap between her two front teeth, which gives her face a bit of asymmetry. She speaks French but with a heavily English accent, and she has that classic rosy complexion with freckles across the bridge of her nose. Then there is the hair. Light brown, straight, a few layers for movement, cascading a little past her shoulders. And the most important part: long bangs that graze her eyebrows, emphasizing big, expressive greenish-blue eyes. She's quite slim and on the tall side, a natural willowy gamine type, an ectomorph born from a family of thinness and wealth.

Once she's done riffling through her Birkin's detritus, she looks right at the camera and says, "Find out anything after seeing what's in the bag? Even when you show it all, you reveal very little." She has a wry look on her face, inviting us to want to know more.

Birkin is not just the inspiration behind one of the most exclusive handbags of all time, but one of the greatest muses of the last hundred years. Her style from the 1960s and '70s solidified her as the real version of an often-overused term: a fashion icon. Born in England but synonymous with the French girl style she helped codify in her adopted home country, she maintained a fierce dedication to her own aesthetic that has charmed and inspired for decades. She is the reason why high-waisted denim with flared hems, fluttery white peasant blouses, Repetto ballet flats, crocheted dresses, and woven baskets as handbags are still worn today; why the French girl style proliferates. She is carefree elegance personified.

Yet Birkin was more than just a well-dressed woman with an unforgettable face and a slew of famous relationships. Over the course of her life, Birkin became a revered actress who appeared in more than seventy films and a musician whose most famous song was banned by the Vatican for its lasciviousness. From the Beatles to Princess Diana, she ran in circles with virtually every celebrity of her lifetime. She birthed three famous daughters with three famous men and was committed to activism from childhood. And yet her life was terrifically complicated. As the heroine of her own story, she doesn't always make the decisions you want her to.

I didn't come to Birkin through the bag but instead as a devout and raging Francophile. My birthday is Bastille Day, the French independence day, so you might call my love for all things French a sort of chicken-and-egg thing. Like Birkin, I lived in Paris at age twenty-one.

Why does any woman move to Paris from another country? The forces that draw us there can of course be as mundane as any of our lives can be. For me it was a kind of test. After studying French for seven years in schools roughly five thousand miles away from Paris, I wanted to go beyond watching New Wave films and buying Petit Écolier dark chocolate cookies and really see if I could hold my own at a French university. I was there for school; Birkin moved for a job. But with France, there's more than that. There's myth, beauty, art, desire, and reinvention. The promise of *joie de vivre*. I wanted to cultivate unbridled insouciance, effortlessly chic style, and a seductive air of mystery.

Jane Birkin always made achieving that seem attainable. When she moved to Paris thirty years before I did, her life instantly came together. I can't say mine quite did. Instead of being assimilated as an instant *Parisienne*, I was deeply aware of all the ways I felt too inelegant, too far from a waif, too heavily American-accented to be mistaken for any kind of native, let alone welcomed into the Gallic fold. I was deeply disappointed that becoming French wasn't so easy; Jane made it seem so accessible. If you were just as open as she seemed to be, or at least embodied her unique brand of *je ne sais quoi* chic, you could have her life too. Over time, I learned that the French girl is merely a construct; there is no monolith, no matter what marketing tells you. French women do indeed get fat and aren't all white and wealthy; there is more nuance there than what has been sold to us.

And there is more to Birkin, too, than what has been sold to us. If I'm going to be perfectly frank, I wrote her off for years. I thought her breathy vocals on Serge Gainsbourg's songs were endearing and her way of wearing shrunken white T-shirts with the necks stretched out to reveal a flash of collarbone was undeniably cool, but she also came across like the glorified accessory to the latest mercurial man in her life. "Men often saw me as their B-side," she once said, and I readily bought into this sentiment because I myself wanted to be the artist, not the muse.

It was only upon researching her that I realized that being a muse was not all she wanted for herself either. It took Birkin until she was around forty years old to assert herself creatively and honestly show the world she was more than an It Girl. Hers was a life full of surprises and contradictions that confront motherhood, sexuality, fame, consent, abuse, respect. It is a legacy that is worth looking at closely. She rarely spoke about her first marriage as a teenager in London to a rapscallion of a husband. In her twenties and thirties, much of her private recollections focused on her romantic relationships and her family life. She liked going out, and she sometimes bought into the public role of being an It Girl, but, particularly as she aged into her thirties and beyond, she was much more concerned with being seen as an artistic force in film and music. And the Hermès bag that is synonymous with her to this day? Never warranted even a sentence of Birkin's personal writing.

Birkin had chosen France as her home in the 1960s; in the fifty years that followed, she managed to become synonymous with their culture. So, in late 2023, I moved to Paris for a few months for research; I interviewed Birkin's friends and acquaintances, toured her former homes, and ate at some of her favorite restaurants. I spent time in the archives of magazine publishers and fashion designers. I read hundreds of articles and watched TV news segments and listened to radio interviews with her. I watched countless movies; I read books about her romantic partners and family. I went to an Hermès workshop to see a Birkin being meticulously and painstakingly crafted. And, of course, I visited the cemetery in Paris where she is buried.

When Jane Birkin died in 2023, there was an outpouring of emotion from her adopted home country, memorializing what she meant for their culture. President Emmanuel Macron called her "a French icon." Anne Hidalgo, the mayor of Paris, dubbed her "the most Parisian of the English." As the French newspaper *Libération* wrote in her obituary, "Was it the British accent, *so charming* but a bit annoying at the same time? Or the fact that beyond her sweetness, it allowed we [*sic*], the French, to remind our frenemies the English, that we were the ones who spotted her talent?"

The papers got it right: She was an icon. But it took immersing myself in her world to appreciate what that meant, how she did it, and its lasting influence on the world. Finally I could see how she was situated in history and culture, and how Jane Birkin deserved, at long last, to be at the center of her own narrative.

The Birkin I aim to capture is someone more fully realized than the fantasy that surrounded her. The portrait that emerged for me was a woman who merited a clear but not obsequious telling of her story. Being a gorgeous young thing is part of her legacy, but far from the whole picture. That tension between who she was to the world and who she was to herself fuels a compelling story of a woman who both pushed into and pulled away from how the world regarded her talent and her desires.

The term "It Girl" is a shorthand for her unique brand of fame, but it's just the beginning of who Jane Birkin really was.

CHAPTER ONE

Eccentric, Glamorous, and All Quite Brilliant

Before she was French, she was English.

Jane Birkin was born during a particularly bleak postwar time in British history, when rations were common and luxury was not. After she was delivered on December 14, 1946—premature at seven and a half months—at the London Clinic in Marylebone, she was kept in a little box on the radiator with another baby, both covered in a damp cloth because the clinic lacked an incubator. England had one of its worst winters in recorded history, with heavy snow, coal shortages, and blackouts.

It may not have been the most auspicious start to her life, but ultimately the Birkin children—Jane, the middle child, was raised along with older brother Andrew and younger sister Linda—were largely insulated from the hardships that others of their era faced. Birkin's father, David, was from a Nottingham family that owned Birkin Lace, which had manufactured the fabric since 1825. Their curtains were wildly popular in the Victorian era and had made the family business successful and generationally wealthy. There was some nobility in the family line, too, as David Birkin was related to the Duke of Bedford on his maternal side. They weren't landed gentry—there were no aristocratic titles or castles—and while they weren't the richest or grandest family by any means, they lived among and were well-connected to the upper classes. (Jane Birkin even once met Queen Elizabeth II as a child at the lace factory and presented her with flowers.)

Birkin's mother, Judy Campbell, was a well-known stage actress who had made her debut as a teenager. She was beautiful in a Golden Age of Hollywood way, with dark curls, pale skin, and an elegant jawline. She became muse to the celebrated playwright Noël Coward, touring in his productions of *Present Laughter*, *This Happy Breed*, and *Blithe Spirit*. Campbell's parents—Jane's grandparents—were also actors. They never had a great deal of money but made up for that with their social capital. When Campbell was single, she lived in a flat with two actress friends: Winston Churchill's daughter Sarah Churchill, who would later become Birkin's godmother, and David Birkin's cousin Penelope Dudley-Ward (who had the odd-sounding but affectionate nickname of "Pemple").

David Birkin was a military man and a secret agent during World War II whose missions were even the subject of a book by Tim Spicer called *A Dangerous Enterprise*. Pemple adored her cousin and thought Campbell was a ravishing young woman. She introduced them at her daughter Tracy Reed's christening ceremony in 1942, where Birkin and Campbell were both present as the child's godparents. Their first date was to see the movie *Dr. Jekyll and Mr. Hyde*.

David Birkin and Judy Campbell married on November 12, 1943, in the same church where they had met at the christening. The wedding wasn't lavish but not exactly wartime austere either. A newsreel called *Movietone News* covered the ceremony, showing them as a dashing and stylish couple, even when filmed in black-and-white. Campbell wore a white lace gown with long sleeves and a matching pillbox hat, carrying a branch blooming with white flowers. Her very tall, very thin new husband looked somehow all the more handsome while sporting an eye patch with his formal suit and slicked-back hair. (He had been through dozens of operations for eye and lung issues following a sinus operation that had gone wrong when he was a teenager.) They did not have a proper honeymoon, as both were busy: He was still fighting in the war on a gunboat, and she was on tour as Noël Coward's leading lady.

The children came shortly thereafter. Andrew was born in December 1945, Jane almost exactly a year later, and Linda in 1950.

After a few early years spent on a farm in rural Berkshire, they were raised in the London borough of Chelsea, in a big Victorian home on Cheyne Gardens. The parents weren't really hands-on types—the feeding, the changing of diapers, the nap times, all the hallmarks of life with a newborn, were outsourced to a series of nannies. Nor were they very affectionate—her mother, Birkin said, was too glamorous for that. Their parenting style was in that respect reminiscent of an earlier Edwardian era, with children staying in their own domains and remaining better seen than heard.

Birkin and her brother behaved like twins; they were inseparable and would be for their entire lives. Linda often complained about being left out. Later on, if those two thought about their childhoods, they didn't think of Linda at all. Andrew called her "an intruder, disguised as our sister." The two Birkin daughters had forced proximity, sharing a bedroom on the top floor of their Chelsea house, where they moved in 1956. But there was an emotional distance between them, with Linda claiming that Jane was always the one to seek out attention. "She had a taste for drama. A very strong taste," Linda wrote in 2024. "Even when we were little, if her lips were chapped by the cold, she would squeeze them together with all her strength until they bled, then she would show her wound. She needed an audience."

In that sense, Birkin took after her mother. Campbell was never a star but rather a respected working actress. However, she put her steady stage career aside while she raised children. In the postwar baby boom period, when wifely domesticity was fetishized, there was little precedent for women to try to pursue their own lives along with parenting. And in Britain's upper classes, it was not the norm for a woman to have a job outside the home. David Birkin loved his wife but did not care for show business, thinking it a silly career. At home, Judy Campbell remained a diva, with strong opinions and a raging intellect. For as long as she could remember, Jane found it hard to be the gangly daughter of a professionally beautiful person. Next to her mother, she felt downright mousy. "She said I was lucky to be like a mouse, because people would take care of me. She used to say that if you're dark and six foot and glamorous like she was that no one asks if you're all right, but with me they're always concerned I'm about to faint, so they look after me. I suppose I am lucky like that," Birkin remembered.

Despite a certain chilliness in the emotional register of the family home, Birkin later said David and Judy were great parents for encouraging curiosity and intellectual interests: *Richard III*, poetry, P. G. Wodehouse, Proust, drawing. They went to the cinema to see big MGM movies and British kitchen sink dramas, a film movement showing all the realism and grit of postwar British life. Creativity was a Birkin family pursuit, and Jane and her siblings were given free rein to concentrate on it. One summer, the three children created their own club, the Cat Club, brainstorming whimsical ways to make money: collecting wildflowers to sell them in bunches; gathering blackberries and raspberries; foraging mushrooms. There was a freedom and old-fashioned playfulness in which the Birkin siblings were allowed to fully indulge.

Acting, in particular, was an artistic pastime they all enjoyed together. Judy Campbell likened the Birkins to another famous family of performers, the Redgraves. It wasn't uncommon for the entire household to put on a show. On Boxing Day when Birkin was fourteen, they staged an original holiday play. The plot was abstract, seemingly something to do with a bird being mistaken for a turkey, although the general merriment was more the point than anything else. Jane's mother did her father's makeup, Andrew directed the scenes, and a family friend was on lighting. This was perhaps Birkin's earliest acting performance. She had a single line—"It's beginning to snow"—which she delivered with a serious intonation as someone threw confetti in the air to emulate snowflakes.

The family had a cottage on the Isle of Wight in the English Channel, with a small, slightly rocky strip of beach bordered by lush, tall grasses. Birkin in particular loved spending time there; she collected shells by day and hosted moonlit evening picnics. More creativity bloomed in that environment. Her parents, sister, brother, and she all made a home movie in the early 1960s called *The Pirate*, in which her father played a pirate who kidnapped Jane and Linda, subsequently saved by Andrew. Andrew later used the setting to make a home movie of his own, filmed on his 8mm camera with a teen-centered plot that involved a beautiful young girl who eventually dies of leukemia. He had wanted to cast his friend Hayley Mills, the star of *The Parent Trap*, whose actor father John Mills had briefly met Judy Campbell during the war. She was out of town filming an actual movie for Disney and couldn't do it, so Andrew cast Jane as a love interest of his best friend.

While the Isle of Wight was her most beloved place, it also ended up being where Birkin felt most isolated. For primary school, she was educated at Miss Ironside's School in Kensington in London, then at age twelve was sent to the all-girls Upper Chine School on the Isle of Wight. Birkin said it had been her idea to go away to boarding school because all her friends were also doing so, but to say she disliked the experience was an understatement. "I spent three miserable, cowardly, sad, ordinary years at school on the Isle of Wight," she wrote in her journal, later published under the name *Munkey Diaries*, which she began writing in 1957 at age ten. (The "Munkey" in question was a soft stuffed monkey dressed like a jockey, which she carried with her everywhere, even into adulthood.) "I dared neither to laugh, nor to be revolutionary, nor individual, nor original, I conformed exactly to my state of a child who wants to please the teacher." She spent a lot of time crying in the bathroom and writing maudlin poems with titles like "Jealousy." The same-sex environment heightened her insecurities. "I suffered a lot because of my physique," she said. "The others said I was half boy, half girl. I had no breasts, not even a developing bosom." She was kicked by a horse named Nugget and had to wear a cast for several weeks, and she was bullied for that too.

Immersed in misery and unable to leave campus without permission, Birkin tried to run away on two different occasions. She was caught both times. Another time she tried making herself sick by eating gravel on the tennis court to see if she could get sent home. All her efforts were fruitless. Boarding school only emphasized the worst part about her home life—coldness—and lacked the creativity and artistic freedom in which her parents did excel. She was ambivalent at best about studying and grades. After two or three years she left to go back to London in 1961, and moved into her old bedroom.

At that age, her diaries were filled with musings that wouldn't be out of place in any young-adult novel about a gangly girl wanting to feel grown-up: feeling excited after buying her first lipstick; admonishing herself to do "I must increase my bust" exercises a hundred times per day; wearing a bra even though she didn't have much need for one; her relief when she finally got her period. "I'm the same as everyone else," she wrote. She wondered a great deal about fitting in, speculating in her diary whether she should try to be more overtly sexy by wearing tight skirts and stockings like the older girls. This phase was potent but short-lived. Later in life, she would embrace being a tomboy, saying, "I've never really seen myself as a girl. I see myself in roles of girls disguised as boys."

While she was growing up, even her mother told her she looked boyish. "When people said to me, 'Are you Judy Campbell's daughter?' and I said, 'Yes,' they said, 'Oh, well you don't really look like her,'" Birkin said in an interview, sounding like she had a good sense of humor about having a gorgeous mother whom she did not resemble. Pop culture loves a story of a siren of a daughter whose beauty outshines the woman who birthed her, but there is a particularly fraught dynamic for the daughters who are deemed more homely than their moms, even if this problem was arguably in Birkin's head. In truth, she was never some ugly duckling who later would turn into a swan; her naturally thin body type simply did not reflect the curvaceous sexiness that was the beauty standard of that time.

As a young teenager, Birkin was slowly figuring out her own version of femininity. The way she dressed during that era was the prototype of what would become her signature style: striped sailor shirts worn with jeans, gingham bikinis, navy peacoats, oversize black sunglasses, scarves or bows tied in her hair. And she began exploring in other ways too. She began to experiment with a few sips of cider, maybe an occasional hit off a joint, and talking to boys, usually friends of friends, at parties. But her budding sexuality was hesitant and innocent at first.

By the time she was fifteen and living back at home, there was a neighbor who lived in an apartment overlooking her room across the street. She found him artsy and cute, and her sister Linda invented a code—"It's raining"—if he was out on his balcony. Birkin would practice ballet in his view to try to get his attention. One day Linda said it was raining, so Birkin went outside to pretend to draw. She heard his voice for the first time—realizing he had a New Zealand accent—and when he turned, she could see he was not her age, but rather an adult, maybe even forty years old. Despite that age difference, she asked her father if she could go to his place, and he said yes because he reasoned he could see her from the house. He must have known he was a fully grown if not middle-aged man who had some romantic intention with his adolescent daughter. The ease with which he allowed Jane to go over to this man's home is unsettling, but it does set the stage for her blithe view on age-gap relationships later on. Her neighbor poured her wine and kissed her behind the front door where her father couldn't see them. She was a hopeless romantic and smitten. "I really do love him; I think about him day and night, it is such a marvelous thing to love someone so much. He told me he feels the same," she wrote in her diary.

By the next year, her neighbor had moved to a basement apartment in a different neighborhood, but she would still visit. One evening they ate ratatouille. He drank whiskey and she drank too much red wine. She lay down, and he tried to get on top of her. She said she was on her period and he responded that it didn't matter to him, which she found disgusting. "I ran away," she wrote in her diary, failing to add whether he had responded with aggression or she was able to just leave. She reached home only to be greeted by her father, who was angry at her for coming home so late and said an apology was not sufficient. Jane went upstairs and swallowed as much children's aspirin as she could find. At four in the morning, Linda found her sister deathly pale and called to her mother. They took her to the hospital, where her stomach was pumped. Afterward, her mother slapped her. Later, at home, she wrote a poem called "Suicide Lost" ("I cried for something I would never have"). Jane

Birkin never described the incident with her neighbor as assault, and she mentioned offhandedly in later interviews that her first love was from New Zealand. But what transpired that night was enough to make a dramatic and lasting impression on the young girl and perhaps foreshadow further romantic hardships.

CHAPTER TWO

Can't You Make an Effort?

Birkin's family hatched a plan for her to move forward, an old-fashioned one that could have been relevant in Jane Austen's era. She would live at home in London, where she would become a debutante at age seventeen or eighteen, making her formal entrée in the social circuit of the well-off and wellborn. From there she would marry into a wealthy family, like any other nice, respectable, but ultimately unambitious girl of her social class. But in 1963 she was only sixteen, and a coming-out ball was a few years away. Birkin lacked a job and still wasn't interested in school. Her parents needed to find something to keep her busy—and to keep up appearances. So they sent her to Paris for a few months.

Paris was meant to serve as a kind of finishing school for Birkin, which was a normal trajectory for young women of her ilk at that time. It would give her a bit of culture and something to do before she settled into the serious business of finding a husband back in London. The trip was like a vestige of the Grand Tour, on which monied young women in centuries past would be sent to continental Europe to see a bit of the world outside of Great Britain and amass some style and furnishings for their future stately homes.

Birkin was not initially thrilled with the idea. For the self-proclaimed tomboy, going there felt like punishment. She was most comfortable on a windy beach, improvising plays with her family. Comparing it to another version of boarding school, she announced to her parents, "It's bad enough being sent to the Isle of Wight, so if you send me to France, I'll kill myself!" But off she went.

Birkin lived in Paris with a group of young women in the home of a woman named Madame P., also known as Countess Puget. Puget regularly hosted small groups of English girls on boulevard Lannes in the 16th arrondissement in the old-monied, western edge of Paris, where they were given skills to become worldly-enough wives, mothers, and hostesses. There the girls received instruction on the French lifestyle: cooking lessons to perfect chocolate truffles, trips to the flea market, visits to the French Impressionist paintings at the Jeu de Paume, and, of course, practice conversing in French. From the very beginning, Birkin was bad at mastering the language. Her heavy English accent and her "franglais" would be a source of endearment, amusement, and derision (sometimes all at once) for the rest of her life.

Her initial relationship to Paris was mixed. She liked Renoir's paintings but "not his very fat, pink, nude ladies—talk about spare tires!" and she enjoyed the cuisine of the city—"stuffed with garlic," she wrote in her diary approvingly. She enjoyed the thrill of being able to buy a bra at a lingerie store that was open at 9 p.m., and thought the Gothic Catholic cathedrals were impressive, even if she found their services to be long and boring. She also liked the pace of Paris, where people took long lunches and sat in cafés talking for hours. While the city and its locals were vibrant, their personalities were more clipped and their attitudes more confrontational than in London. Despite her initial misgivings, her family could tell she begrudgingly enjoyed herself, because she would send animated letters home with stories of her misadventures.

During Birkin's time abroad, she was more entranced by her solo excursions than with forging any lifelong bonds with the other women staying with Madame P. She did meet a boy around her age named Bertrand with whom she developed a platonic friendship, showing her what that sort of connection with a man could look like. They drove around the city together—past the Arc de Triomphe one day, to the castle at Versailles another day—and rowed in little boats in the Bois de Boulogne. It sounds like a perfect romance, but it was instead just a friendship. This possibility was a revelation for Birkin. Instead of obsessing over whether they would kiss, she was relieved to be able to speak freely about intimacies she felt shy about sharing with anyone else, such as how many affairs they were supposed to have before they got married.

Birkin's first brush with infamy came during that French sojourn. She discovered she lived on the same block as legendary singer Edith Piaf, who sadly passed away in the South of France in October 1963, during Birkin's time in Paris. There was an outpouring of mourning for the star, with impromptu vigils on the streets. Amid this chaos on her block, someone in that crowd mistakenly called out Birkin as Françoise Hardy. Hardy was a popular French singer of the era associated with *yéyé*, a type of bubblegum pop music. Birkin, with her long bangs and brownish-blond hair, bore a resemblance to Hardy. She was flattered enough that she recorded the experience in her diary with some disbelief. Hardy was famous—and famously cool. Birkin still felt like a kid, even if Hardy was only three years older. Hardy had a career! And those signature white boots . . .

Birkin was likely also mistaken for Hardy because they both stood out in Paris for how they dressed. When Birkin arrived, her style could be described as eclectic but innocent. Her hair was dyed a shade or two lighter than her medium-brown natural color, and she wore fitted knit tops and short skirts. She looked like a teenager trying to keep up with the latest trends at home, but not any kind of fashion pioneer. Her youthful British aesthetic was far from the understated and elegant style dominant in France, even for young women.

In terms of youth culture and fashion, Birkin's native London was far ahead of Paris. At that time, French youth still looked reined in compared to Brits like Birkin. Young Parisian women dressed *soignée*—that is, elegantly, like younger versions of their mothers. Everything had to be immaculate. "French women start with the same ingredients, but they make better use of them," said Birkin. "They were always so beautifully turned out with their velvet headbands and clip-on pearls, a scarf casually tossed over their shoulder." The French woman's dual mastery of allure and control was part of what made Paris the kind of place a family would want their slightly directionless daughter to come of age.

Birkin returned from her Parisian stay, arriving at Waterloo Station at age seventeen, in 1964. "It felt very strange being in London again, the grey buildings and towering brick. I felt very small and insignificant," she wrote. The first person who greeted her back at home was Elda, her family's au pair from Italy. That night after dinner, Birkin went to her bedroom and stared into the mirror. She wrote that she thought she looked dowdy. Even if she resembled Françoise Hardy, it wasn't pronounced enough. What she saw in her reflection didn't match the bold way she wanted the world to see her. She wanted to be noticed. So she started by cutting her own hair, making her bangs more pronounced. The next day, Birkin went to Woolworths on King's Road for mascara and lipstick, tight jeans, and a striped jersey shirt to further develop the way she looked toward something less schoolgirl and more theatrical and *au courant*.

The energy in the British youth movement at that time was infectious, and Birkin fully embraced the moment. She would while away afternoons at cafés on King's Road watching people drive their convertibles by or, on busy Saturdays, walk around Chelsea wearing the shortest miniskirt she could get her hands on and basking in any male attention it brought her. The year 1964 was the beginning of Great Britain's Youthquake, when attitudes around aesthetics and social mores were changing unilaterally. In April 1966, *Time* magazine named London "the Swinging City." Every decade had a defining city, the article stated, whether it was fin de siècle Vienna or Paris in the 1920s or Weimar Berlin or postwar New York City. "Today it is London, a city steeped in tradition, seized by change, liberated by affluence, graced by daffodils and anemones, so green with parks and squares that, as the saying goes, you can walk across it on grass," *Time* wrote. The change came at the right time for England, some needed liveliness after years of postwar austerity. (Food rationing in the UK, for example, went on beyond the end of World War II, past Birkin's birth in late 1946, until 1954.)

Teenagers like Birkin—and people in their twenties—were central to that culture shift toward the national fetishization of all things youthful. The Youthquake was a renaissance era, a nationwide exhale of relief after the war and a recognition of a new generation starting to come of age. It was an infusion into the country of carefree, nearly manic energy that showed not merely in social mores loosening, but also in the clothes people wore, the kinds of films that were made, the sort of music that was popular, the literature of the moment, and the art that represented the times.

That cultural shift very much included fashion designers such as Mary Quant, known for her crayon-colored shift dresses, and Barbara Hulanicki, whose Biba bohemian dresses were often shades of rust and jewel tones with art nouveau–style prints. "Where female fashions of the previous decades had emphasised the bust and hips, Hulanicki's short designs focused on the wearer's legs. Her outfits best accommodated women whose under-fed post-war bodies allowed them to squeeze into unforgiving dresses (stretch fabrics were yet to be invented)" was how the Victoria and Albert Museum's costume department described the Biba client. Their clothes fit Birkin, both aesthetically and physically. These designers were local—some, like Mary Quant, within walking distance from Birkin's home—and their designs clearly inspired her.

After an adolescence of being bullied because of her body, Birkin benefited from the changing trends. In the 1960s, the female ideal in fashion became associated with Twiggy and Jean Shrimpton, who were coltish and didn't look at all like the patrician models who had dominated the 1950s, as well as the actress Julie Christie, whom Birkin loved for often looking eclectic and a bit haphazard. "You'd see photos of Julie Christie coming down her front steps wearing a raincoat over her pajamas with gum boots, spectacles perched at the end of her nose. It was so unpretentious—and so very English," she later recalled. Teenage Jane had, by this point, developed a sharp eye for fashion, and part of her aesthetic drive was that she didn't want anything to look too perfect or too planned out.

Her cohort's youthful way of dressing referenced fashions of past decades and centered on vintage stores. As much as Birkin enjoyed shopping along King's Road, if she wanted to be a style authority and really stand out, she had to dig a little deeper. She couldn't just buy Biba, for example, but needed to buy the dresses Biba's Barbara Hulanicki was inspired by. Prior to this time in the mid-1960s, buying secondhand clothing was something one did only out of economic necessity. But for young women like Birkin, who could afford to purchase designer clothes, patronizing charity shops was a conscious decision. It was a nod to British eccentricity and the original bohemians of the early twentieth century, and a way of showing a different kind of national pride, mixing the English rose aristocratic type with more of a working-class element.

Around this time, Birkin bought a Portuguese basket at Berwick Street Market, near the West End, where all the theaters were. She used the basket to carry everything she needed—cash, makeup, diary—albeit in a disorganized jumble. (Sigmund Freud, who thought that a woman's purse could be seen as a substitute for her genitals and riffling through it represented masturbation, would have had a field day.) Using a woven basket as her daily bag was a quirky choice, but it would become her signature accessory for the next thirty years, beloved and imitated by fans as her image became more ubiquitous along with her fame. With her bangs and eyeliner and enormous, bumbling energy, she had a look and a presence that were becoming instantly recognizable. She was of the moment, yet didn't look like anyone else, fusing British Youthquake miniskirts and knee-high hosiery with peasant blouses that nodded to bohemian culture in the United States and ballerina flats reminiscent of the Repetto or Chanel brands that were ubiquitous in Paris.

Birkin's mother, who often liked to change ensembles three times a day, would have preferred her daughter to look more pulled together, to wear more ladylike styles than blue jeans with skinny ribbed knit sweaters tucked into them, or primary-colored dresses hemmed to the upper thigh. Her mother would take one look at Birkin's outfits and ask, "Can't you make an effort?" Nor was her father a fan. He told her the mix of mascara and eye shadow she piled on made her look like a cross between Cleopatra and a prostitute. Birkin was trying to look avant-garde, like the American model Peggy Moffitt, whose graphic, geometric eye makeup was inspired by Japanese Kabuki theater. For a privileged girl like Birkin, playing with style was a way to gently fight against rigid class ideals—and annoy her wealthy parents in the process. It wasn't her conscious motivation, though—if anything, she was still very much seeking her parents' approval. In her diary, she confessed that when her father told her she looked like a tart, it hurt her feelings.

In the summer of 1964, after her return from Paris, Birkin and her father went to Italy for a month. After visits to Venice and Florence, they stayed in Rome. Her father's cousin Pemple was there with her husband, Carol Reed, who was directing *The Agony and the Ecstasy* with Charlton Heston. They visited him on set at the Cinecittà Studios; Birkin found it spectacular. "I asked Carol whether he thought I had a chance as an actress," she told an interviewer years later. "And he said, 'That depends if the camera falls in love with you.'"

She concluded from her visit to Italy that there would be no debutante debut in her future; instead, she wanted to follow in her mother's footsteps and act, even though her father thought she should try going to art school. Birkin's mother had largely put her acting career on hold when she got married and had three children, but the handful of times Birkin witnessed her mother onstage, such as her 1962 turn in George Bernard Shaw's *Heartbreak House* and, later that year, alongside Vanessa Redgrave in *As You Like It*, filled her with inspiration and admiration for the craft. Her mother was particularly supportive of Birkin trying out for roles, likely nostalgic for the days of being a young actress herself.

Determined to be of assistance, Judy Campbell sought out information about productions looking for young actors and new faces and helped her daughter rehearse for an audition for *The Prime of Miss Jean Brodie*. For the audition, a seventeen-year-old Birkin showed up in a dress she had bought for her trip to Italy and a rose her father had pinned on her for luck. She confided in her diary that she felt overdressed and childish. All the other girls were wearing T-shirts and jeans, fresh from acting classes. Birkin had been discouraged from taking acting classes by her mother's friends, who thought she would be better as a raw talent. "I went to the wrong theater," Birkin wrote, "and found myself auditioning for a part as a deaf girl in Graham Greene's play *Carving a Statue*." She didn't know the text. "A man with extraordinary blue eyes said: 'It doesn't matter—she's perfect.' It was Graham Greene." Birkin got the part. She always suspected she was cast because her character had to be carried across the stage, and she was the lightest actress of the bunch and therefore the easiest to pick up. It was a small role, with dramatic impact: Her character was crushed by a bus and died in the final act.

Carving a Statue started in Brighton and then went on to the Haymarket Theatre in the West End in September 1964. The play was largely dismissed as a minor work. The *New York Times* wrote, "It is a heavy-hearted shaggy dog story about an old sculptor who has spent the last fifteen years carving a statue of one of Mr. Greene's favorite characters, God." Despite this, the role was critical in setting Birkin on the path to becoming a professional actress.

From there, her career rolled toward stardom. In 1965 she was featured in the *Daily Mail*'s roundup of "Class of '65—50 Women to Keep an Eye On," which also included the singers Nico and Marianne Faithfull. And despite the middling reviews, both the play and Birkin were draws. Among the audiences who came to see her perform *Carving a Statue* was the actor Michael Crawford (who would, decades later, originate the role of the Phantom in Andrew Lloyd Webber's *Phantom of the Opera*). He recommended Birkin to the director Richard Lester, who cast her in a part in *The Knack . . . and How to Get It* as Motorbike Girl. It was Birkin's first appearance in a film, albeit something of a walk-on role. *The Knack . . . and How to Get It* won the Palme d'Or at the Cannes Film Festival in 1965 and helped kick off the British New Wave in cinema. Birkin also appeared in a mid-'60s commercial for Cadbury's Bar Six, playing a young woman who parks to buy the candy from a vending machine but doesn't pay for parking. She uses her charm to divert the parking officer's attention, offering him one. Birkin was far from a household name, but she was becoming recognizable for her image as the quintessential Swinging Sixties girl.

She also had started to make friends with others in the business, such as Gabrielle Lewis, Michael Crawford's future wife. She was a

DJ at the hip Pickwick Club at the time and would become one of Birkin's best friends for life. Then there was Charlotte Rampling, who also had a tiny role in *The Knack . . . and How to Get It*. Even the Beatles were part of her proudly young, proudly British social circle. Andrew Birkin, who had gone into the film world and was working with Stanley Kubrick on *2001: A Space Odyssey*, introduced them while he was serving as an assistant director on the Beatles' film *Magical Mystery Tour*. Birkin was photographed with Ringo Starr and George Harrison in the '60s in the South of France. In her diaries she wrote, "Lunch with J. Lennon, very nice." No further description needed.

On a night out at the Ad Lib Club in Leicester Square when she was still just seventeen, she met Roman Polanski. The Polish-born director was a young and hot new name in the industry; his first feature-length film, *Knife in the Water*, had been nominated for the Academy Award for Best Foreign Language Film. Polanski encouraged her to try out for the character Mary Rose Byng-Bentall in the upcoming West End musical comedy *Passion Flower Hotel*. She took his advice and auditioned, landing the part. For the role, Birkin sang a silly song about increasing her bust size.

The production's composer was John Barry, who was famous for having written and arranged the scores to the James Bond films *Dr. No* and *To Russia with Love*. When they first met, Birkin recalled feeling nervous around him, as if every question she asked about how he composed was dumb. "I thought he was very good-looking," she wrote. "I passed him on the stairs and thought I would nearly die if he spoke to me."

Though she was a burgeoning star in the Youthquake scene, Birkin was still only seventeen, and a somewhat reserved seventeen at that, considering her proximity to fame. She drank and routinely stayed out all night but didn't partake of hard drugs or pills. Birkin didn't get the appeal of having drugs running through her veins; they frightened her. And she didn't have very much experience with men either. Apart from a few boys her age she met at parties, and the manipulative experience with her neighbor, she remained largely inexperienced with dating. She was still very much a virgin when she starred in *Passion Flower Hotel*, but Barry entranced her. He was an accomplished and attractive man-about-town who was known for his quick, self-deprecating wit. Barry has never said publicly what exactly he saw in Birkin, whether it was her beauty or her talent or her rising stardom or her innocence—or some combination of all those traits—but the attraction was mutual and they started dating.

In terms of experience, they were not on equal ground. Barry was thirty years old and divorced, and he already had two children, one of whom lived in Sweden with an ex-girlfriend of his; he rarely saw either of them. Birkin claimed he told her all about it in the first few hours of knowing him, which to her was proof he had nothing to hide. "I sort of accepted it like a child accepts everything as normal," she wrote. The very idea that Barry had a past at all intimidated her, though. It's not resentment that comes through in her writing; Birkin instead struggles with her own insecurity, trying to understand how he could love her after dating a blond and beautiful Swede. Perhaps that was what he liked about her: that she cared about how he felt and not how he treated her. In her youthful naïveté and sweet spirit, Birkin was not a challenging partner. Instead, she longed for him and wished to be understood by him. Or, in stronger words, she was a little desperate for his attention.

Their dynamic was all too reminiscent of a child throwing a fit in order to get noticed by a parent. Birkin's sister remembered that after some kind of petty fight—the root of which no one could recall—Birkin went into the middle of the street outside the family home in Chelsea hoping that Barry would chase after her and threaten to run her over with his Jaguar. "To her great disappointment, he never came to get her or run her over. So she pretended to be drunk and staggered back home," Linda Birkin said. "She played the martyr to perfection. She was aware she was not easy to live with."

The difference in age and life experience certainly didn't stop their relationship. But things progressed physically only to a point; Birkin would not have sex with him before there was a ring on her finger. "I was brought up to think that you should never sleep with anyone unless they ask you to marry them, so thankfully he popped the question, and that was somehow alright," she later said. They had known each other for six months when he proposed. She was swept up in the idea of romance and said yes; her family, however, was less enthusiastic. David Birkin wanted to go to court to forbid his daughter to marry Barry. There was a tense discussion between Birkin's father and her beau in the garden of the Birkins' Chelsea home—two men negotiating the life of a teenage girl. Her brother, who shared a dislike of Barry, filmed it. "You can see my father trying to postpone the date, you see John Barry winning, Andrew grimacing, and me following John Barry through the house to his Jaguar E-Type, getting in, with my basket. Three months later I was eighteen, and we were man and wife," she wrote. She married Barry at a simple Chelsea registry office ceremony wearing a white crochet minidress.

Birkin had been ascendant as an actress known to the public since she was seventeen, but now, at the tender age of eighteen, she was half of an artistic power couple. Her earliest appearance in *Vogue* in the August 1966 issue reads, "For the prettiest girls in London, or anywhere, two enchanting evening looks. Both are worn by Jane Birken [*sic*], a disarming young English actress with wide, wondering hazel eyes." She was exactly the kind of woman *Vogue* would cover: young, thin, good-looking, wellborn, in the public eye, quirky-looking but in a way that wasn't hard for their readers to stomach.

Birkin was struggling to transition from girlhood into wifedom, and was having a difficult time trying to be the perfect young bride in the public sphere. She slept with an eyeliner pencil under her pillow so she could apply some at any moment, so as not to be seen by her own husband with what she perceived as "tiny, piggy eyes." She told *Elle* in 2020: "There was such insecurity, it was quite crazy—I spent most of my time trying to look like a fashion tableau." She had fallen for the fairy-tale ideal of romance and marriage, and as a result she closed off her own sense of self. She even got rid of her late grandmother's bird, Polly, which she had inherited. Barry hated the bird and made her choose between the pet and the husband. "And like an idiot," she wrote, "I chose John."

The couple's schedules were challenging; shared time was scant due to their creative projects. Barry was off recording *Thunderball*, another Bond film, all day, and she wouldn't get home from performances of *Passion Flower Hotel* until eleven thirty each night. Still a teen, she was swept up in love, and would arrive home with a burst of energy. He would tell her to be quiet, which would make her cry and feel foolish. She thought it was a positive sign that she wanted to see him so much. She was also, frankly, horny, and Barry didn't always reciprocate. A lack of sex quickly became the norm. "Having to play with yourself when you're married is degrading and I'm beginning to feel bitter," she wrote in her journal.

It was not just that her enthusiasm outpaced his; he could be cruel too. He'd deliver such charmless observations as her eyes were small or that she had too much energy. A lifelong insomniac, Birkin was prescribed sleeping pills during the marriage, which didn't always work. She would cry herself to sleep at night, inert, next to her slumbering new husband.

About six weeks after they married, in November 1965, Birkin returned from a matinee and changed into lingerie, wanting to surprise her husband when he came home. After hours of waiting, she called the restaurant where he had supposedly been dining. They said he had a table for two for 9 p.m. but by then had left hours earlier. She waited for the sound of the elevator stopping at their floor as a signal he was back; he finally came home much later and told her flat out that he had been out with another woman. For a moment she was naïve enough to let herself think it might have been his secretary or a family member. "You don't want me to lie, do you?" he asked, and told her the woman was an actress, a Brigitte Bardot–style buxom blonde who had previously dated Michael Caine. "I can't explain what a slap on the face it was for me. I didn't suspect John of being unfaithful, it wasn't really that, it was just that there I was, dying with cold and crying. . . . J told me to shut up crying and go to bed," she wrote.

Birkin was so devastated by the news of the actress dalliance that she got out of bed and walked into the doorframe, which gave her a black eye. She then went to the kitchen, took eggs out of a bowl and started methodically smashing them into the sink, and subsequently scratched at her own legs until they bled. Then, her rage temporarily exhausted, she got back into bed.

The following day she went to a doctor because she was bleeding before she was due for her period. She told him she felt ghastly and had had a terrible week. The doctor told her it could have been a miscarriage. She fell into deep melancholia, trapped in a miserable marriage that her family had warned her against. A few weeks later, in December 1965, she wrote Barry a letter as a diary entry while he slept. She explained in plaintive language that she felt capable of hurting herself:

"I saw a glass and I knew I would break it and try to cut myself. It doesn't mean I tried to die; I don't want that because I love you and I have so much to live for, but sometimes when you are asleep and I haven't been able to tell you the way I feel, the only crap way I can comfort myself is to sink deep into my skin, so it hurts me and the pain seems to stop."

The root of her pain was loneliness. Even when they were together, even now that they were married, she still felt alone. Birkin, who was still a teenager, was idealistic enough to think that if she expressed how much he was hurting her and showed her love for him clearly, he would change. And yet she could not resist demonstrating that she was still eager to please her husband, promising that she would also try to be more patient with him.

Meanwhile, Birkin's public and professional life continued to flourish. At a party in early 1966, she met Warren Beatty, who flirted with her. "He seems to think I'm funny and interesting for his next film," she wrote. He came to see her in *Passion Flower Hotel* and left at intermission to call the director and producer of the next project to extol Birkin's talent. She was cast in a tiny role as a character billed as Exquisite Thing in Beatty's 1966 movie *Kaleidoscope*. She then appeared in the 1968 psychedelic film *Wonderwall*, in which she played a model named Penny Lane. *Women's Wear Daily* wrote a small profile of her when it came out with the headline "Jane Grows

Up." Her diary entries from that era show a young woman whose world was opening up, filled with mentions of encounters with heavy hitters of the era, from Peter O'Toole to Charlie Chaplin.

Birkin really broke out in a small role in one of the defining films of 1960s England, Michelangelo Antonioni's *Blow-Up*, a thriller set in the fashion world of London. The story was loosely based on the life of British fashion photographer David Bailey (played by David Hemmings). In it, Jane plays the Blonde, one of a pair of gangly teenage groupies who show up at the photographer's studio hoping he'll take pictures of them. Landing the role was more happenstance than a conscious effort for her to channel her talent. She wasn't aware of who Antonioni was when she came to the audition. "I was asked to write my name on a wall, and every three letters, to turn my profile to see if I was photogenic," Birkin recalled in her journals. An Italian assistant was bothering her, and she burst into tears. "Antonioni came and yelled: 'Stop, that's enough. I've seen what I wanted to see.' He wanted to see emotion, and he had."

She trusted Antonioni, who was exacting in every detail of her makeup and costumes. She compared him to an architect. In one of the movie's most memorable scenes, the Blonde and her fellow Brunette groupie both strip naked and wrestle with the photographer, in what comes across as foreplay for a threesome. John Barry was supportive of the role. "[He] told me that I'd never dare show myself naked on set because I always turned the lights out at home. . . . So, just because he'd said that I did dare," she wrote in her journal.

Because of the scene, the Motion Picture Association of America's Production Code Administration refused to give *Blow-Up* its seal of approval. MGM released the movie anyway; it made a huge amount of money—$20 million on a budget of $1.8 million. And its place in movie trivia was forever cemented because it helped end the Hays Code, Hollywood's long-standing censorship system, which had been introduced in the 1930s and advised special care in images like a couple in bed together or "excessive or lustful kissing." Nudity was forbidden.

The film was a phenomenon. It won the Palme d'Or at Cannes;

internationally, there were lines around the block to see it. Birkin underplayed her role in it as a minor character who is just a distraction for the protagonist. And while she was catapulted to new levels of fame, she did not find it led to any starring roles.

She did not seem to dwell on that, instead turning her focus on her role as wife. She wanted a child, both because she wanted to be a mother and because she thought it would help cement her marriage with John Barry. "With a child, I'd be fulfilled," she wrote. "I'd be so much nicer, anyway." Barry's reaction was to buy an apartment in Belgravia near where he lived with Birkin, with the excuse that it was for the quiet he needed to do his work as a composer. "That place," he later told *Mojo* magazine, "created . . . opportunities." Many of their arguments didn't end but rather were mollified by sex. Despite martial tension, Birkin did get pregnant.

On April 7, 1967, twenty-year-old Birkin went into labor. The day was a normal one: She walked down King's Road and went to see her parents. When she got home in the early evening, she and Barry made an early dinner and went to bed—or he did, via sleeping pills. She felt pains like gastroenteritis and got out her copy of Dr. Spock's *Baby and Child Care.* She called the London Clinic, where she had also been born, once her pains—contractions—were about five minutes apart, and they advised she come straight to the hospital. But before she did, she wanted to make sure she was the image of feminine presentability, ironing a dress and putting on makeup before she roused Barry.

Barry was surprisingly present during labor, holding her hands through each contraction. Their daughter was born on April 8, 1967; she weighed seven pounds and had dark, almost black hair and blue eyes. Barry wanted to call the baby Siobhan, but Birkin thought it too similar to Sian, one of his other daughters; they settled on Kate Barry, after a cousin of Birkin's and the musical *Kiss Me, Kate.*

Even with the arrival of their child, things with Barry never regained any kind of smooth footing, not that their relationship had had very much to begin with. They fought constantly, to the point where glasses were broken and shouting matches were the norm. In May of 1967, they went on vacation to Mallorca in an attempt to rekindle any kind of intimacy between them. Birkin mourned the fact that he didn't want to have sex with her. "I want to be desired," she wrote. "But I really only want it from John because I love him and it seems he is destroying me as he has everybody else."

From there, they traveled separately over the summer of 1967. Barry went to Paris to record Renata Tarragó, a classical guitarist, while Birkin went back to London and then to Almería in southern Spain to visit her brother Andrew, who was location-managing the film *Play Dirty* with Michael Caine. Birkin was still in Spain when her father phoned with the news that Barry had left her. Barry had taken off for Rome, and he wasn't alone. Barry never commented on why he didn't tell his wife directly that he was cheating. Rather, he flaunted his infidelity so blatantly that word had spread to Birkin's family, who gathered to care for her.

By August 1967, Birkin officially left Barry. She flew back to London and came to the home she shared with him. "I found John sitting in his armchair, imperious, and when I kicked up a fuss about Rome, he said, 'The time has come for us to go our separate ways,'" she wrote in her diary. She moved back in with her parents, this time with a four-month-old baby in tow. "I think they were secretly relieved." She had almost no money of her own, and even though Barry was supposed to pay her thirty pounds per week as alimony, he never did. She could barely afford diapers for Kate.

At twenty years old, Birkin's life had collapsed, but she wasn't ready to wallow. Instead, she channeled that heartbreak into another adventure. She was in a restaurant on King's Road with a friend when she heard about an audition for a French film, a romantic comedy called *Slogan* from the director Pierre Grimblat. They heard that all the pretty girls in London were flocking to audition for it following casting searches in Rome and Munich. Perhaps escaping London for France was the answer. No matter that Birkin didn't really speak French, or that she had no idea who the lead in the film would be, even though he was supposedly some big star in France. She couldn't remember his name. Serge Bourguignon, or Gainsborough, or something...

CHAPTER THREE

Folie à Deux

Jane Birkin got invited to test for the role in *Slogan*. That was the good news. The bad news was she had taken an instant dislike to the film's star, Serge Gainsbourg. Gainsbourg was a multi-threat musician, songwriter, producer, director, and actor who embodied a certain French national spirit and whose collaborations with other artists remain the stuff of legend. "He's meant to be my lover, but he's so arrogant and snobbish—he absolutely despises me," Birkin said on the telephone to her brother Andrew. In his own memory, "She described him as this ghastly man who was arrogant and made her feel like a worm."

"He did have quite a reputation in France," Birkin said years later, in 2021. "A bit like Lord Byron. Mad, bad, and dangerous to know." Gainsbourg bought into his own myth too. He said, "She was a girl of light, I, a man of shadow. . . ."

Slogan was about a French director of commercials for consumer goods, Serge Fabergé (Gainsbourg, for whom the role was written), who meets a British woman, Evelyne (Birkin, who plays basically herself, basket bag and all), while he's in Venice receiving an award. The two fall in love, but there's a problem: The director has a wife, a child (played by Birkin's daughter, Kate), and another baby on the way back in Paris. Serge's wife leaves him, but Evelyne also ends up leaving the director for an Italian dandy. Emotional pain ensues. It was a farce about the world of advertising and the sex lives of adults based on the director Pierre Grimblat's own life. He had worked on ad campaigns and was married five times to a series of glamorous women.

Birkin was not the first choice for the role; the American-born model Marisa Berenson was. She not only was multilingual but came from a pedigree. Her grandmother was the designer Elsa Schiaparelli, and Berenson herself was a very famous model who'd been discovered by *Vogue*'s Diana Vreeland. But the career of a covergirl was short, and Berenson was at the peak of the industry—she would not commit to an acting career until the early 1970s, when she was cast in *Death in Venice*. So Birkin made inroads with both her experience and her charm. In the casting process, Birkin's self-deprecating humor made her stand out. Grimblat saw her coming down the stairs to her London audition, wearing a miniskirt, and made a comment about her bowlegs. Instead of taking offense or noting his rudeness, she one-upped him, making a joke that if she could have them reset, she'd be the first to pay for the operation. He invited her to fly out to Paris to test for the role with Gainsbourg.

The chemistry read with her prospective costar did not go smoothly. Her French was bad—her accent was strong and she learned her lines phonetically without understanding what they meant. When they read together, Gainsbourg told her, in a backhanded compliment, that he would never have had the nerve to attempt a film in a language that wasn't his own. At one point during the audition, she cried. She was still adrift and emotionally bereft in the wake of her divorce from John Barry; her test with the casually cruel Gainsbourg unsettled her. She returned to London not knowing whether she had the part. Birkin assumed she was not right for the role because she wasn't right for France. But, in spite of his initial sneer, Gainsbourg hadn't vetoed her.

Gainsbourg was famous for his looks—or lack of them, depending on who was discussing the subject. One English-language news segment described him as being in possession of "a face that reminded one commentator of a badly sewn together fire hose." He had jug ears, a long nose, and downward pointing, mournful eyes, the kind of striking face onto which someone can project melancholy, louche appeal, or malevolence. A Rorschach test of a face. He smoked five packs of unfiltered Gitane cigarettes a day—and looked like it. "To see [Gainsbourg and Jane] together is to believe again every romantic novel ever written," the BBC reported in 1970.

France is a country where beauty is discussed rather directly and clinically as a matter of fact, and Gainsbourg was no exception. The French have a term, *jolie laide*, meaning "ugly-pretty"; Gainsbourg was perhaps more accurately ugly-sexy. A journalist for *Marie Claire* asked him in 1968 why pretty girls liked to pair themselves up with ugly men. "They adore me. I don't even have to lift a finger and my phone never stops ringing. Every day there are more love letters in the mail," he said to the reporter. He was also a provocateur par excellence throughout his career. As part of that, he played fast and loose with misogyny. In 1968 he said to *Paris-Presse*, "Equality for women doesn't exist. They're just like rabbits who've had roller skates strapped on their feet. They might be able to pirouette around on them, but they're still rabbits."

His given name was Lucien Ginsburg; Gainsbourg, his chosen last name, was an homage to the eighteenth-century English painter of lush portraits and landscapes Thomas Gainsborough. His parents were both Jewish and had met at a conservatory in Feodosia, a city in Crimea that was part of the Russian Empire. They married there in 1918 but left soon after so Gainsbourg's father could avoid being drafted into the White Army fighting the Russian Revolution of 1917. Crossing the Black Sea into Istanbul, they made their way to Marseille, then settled in Paris in 1921. Serge and his twin sister Liliane, born in 1928, and older sister Jacqueline grew up in a loosely Jewish home near the cabarets and sex workers of the 9th arrondissement. The family wasn't terribly observant; they never went to synagogue and they celebrated Easter, but they also didn't eat cheese and meat from the same plate.

He was just a kid, *un gamin*, a street urchin or a scamp, during the occupation of France by the Nazis and the subsequent liberation. His family was able to stay in Limoges in 1942, which was a free zone and a safe haven for Jews under the Vichy government, although less so under occupation. Then they moved to a safe house near Versailles, just outside Paris. Nevertheless, the family made it through the era and returned to Paris in 1944. During the war, his father, once a concert pianist, was among the population barred from working under the Nuremberg Laws. Into the postwar era, he was only able to get work playing the piano in hotels and restaurants. This was not only an economic struggle for the family, but a blow to the ego that would influence his son's values. Gainsbourg wanted to be the artist his father wasn't able to be; he wanted to resist authority and get rich.

Gainsbourg, like Birkin, had a peripatetic adolescent life. He dropped out of high school before receiving his *baccalauréat* degree; in 1945, he enrolled in art school, first les Beaux-Arts de Paris and then Académie de Montmartre, where he met the Russian aristocratic émigré model Elisabeth "Lize" Levitsky, whom he married in 1951. There was a mandatory military tour of duty, which he would later blame as the source of his alcoholism. It included no proper war or action but did involve visits to brothels and stints of composing music. He also taught art and music at a school near Paris for children who were orphaned because their parents had been murdered during the Holocaust.

During the 1950s, Gainsbourg had been steadily building a music career in Paris, first playing the piano and working in cabarets, then recording his own music and composing it for other French artists. It was traditional French music, *chanson française*, which can be difficult for modern speakers of the English language to take to as it is notoriously wordy and gets by on lyricism more than rhythm and melody. In the mid-1960s heyday of saccharine-sweet *yéyé* pop music, Gainsbourg found greater notoriety, writing the famous singer France Gall's "Poupée de cire, poupée de son" as well as a controversial hit for her called "Les sucettes" ("Lollipops" in English, or perhaps more literally "Suckers"). The song was risqué, to say the least, with references to sugar dripping down the throat and some homophones with the words "pennies" and "penis," which sound quite similar in a French accent. And Gall wore a schoolgirl uniform at least once while performing it.

Gainsbourg was clear about his desire to mold young female artists. He told the teen magazine *Mademoiselle Âge Tendre* (whose title translates to the rather camp-sounding *Miss Tender Age*) that

"I'd like to discover a 12 or 13 year old girl—no older—and find a style for her. If necessary, I'll have thousands of auditions. She'll have to be very beautiful, of course. I'd be a kind of Pygmalion to her, create a character in the world of song."

Gainsbourg had gained a reputation as a songwriter who was nimble with lyrics, bawdy but clever, and Brigitte Bardot, the bombshell blonde from the South of France, became his muse. Bardot was the superstar for whom the term "sex kitten" was coined. In reality, though, she was shy and bulimic and extremely aware of her own persona as something people, and men in particular, desired to own.

Bardot had sung songs Gainsbourg had written, but in autumn of 1967 he was called in to help work on original songs for an upcoming New Year's Eve special. He penned "Initials BB" and "Comic Strip" for her. One evening in December 1967, he was struck with inspiration for a duet called "Bonnie and Clyde," a song equal parts hopeful and sad telling the story of the infamous outlaw couple of the Great Depression and no doubt inspired by Arthur Penn's 1967 film with Warren Beatty and Faye Dunaway. Gainsbourg and Bardot performed together on the special, lip-syncing in full 1930s regalia as the outlaw duo. Their chemistry was palpable through the screen. They released an album, also called *Bonnie and Clyde*, on January 2, 1968. The record was a true collaboration, and featured Gainsbourg not just composing laconic bass lines but writing dreamy vocals for both of them. It was an artistic high point, with "Bonnie and Clyde" becoming an instant hit and one of the most famous songs either of them made.

After getting divorced from Levitsky in the late 1950s, Gainsbourg had married a second time, in 1964, to Françoise-Antoinette "Béatrice" Pancrazzi, the daughter of a rich industrial family, and had a daughter named Natacha in that same year. He and Pancrazzi divorced in 1966, so he was technically single when he was writing love songs for Bardot, but he and Pancrazzi had their second child, Paul, in 1968, so the relationship could charitably be called complicated. Meanwhile, Bardot had married Gunter Sachs, a wealthy German, in July 1966 after a weeklong engagement. He was an international playboy, the kind of globe-trotting partier who flew to his Las Vegas wedding to Bardot on a plane owned by Edward Kennedy. They were all indulging in their own impulsive decisions.

At some point while working on *Le Bardot Show* and *Bonnie and Clyde*, in a tangled web of sex and commitments and champagne and rehearsals followed by nightcaps, Bardot and Gainsbourg started an affair. They thought they were being discreet, but rumors swirled around the Paris demimonde that they were in love. Gainsbourg had a critically beloved hit song with "Bonnie and Clyde," yet he was turning forty while living with his parents or in a former maid's quarters with shared bathrooms while his own home was being renovated. Bardot left Paris to film the Western *Shalako* in England and Spain with Sean Connery. She phoned Gainsbourg while on location in southern Spain, and they had long talks about whether he should come to Málaga to visit her. She claimed to be bored, but she wasn't alone—she was accompanied by the Amazons, what everyone called the crew of attractive girlfriends and secretaries who rarely left her side. Bardot and Gainsbourg decided against him coming to visit because she was being followed by reporters and she especially didn't want to attract a scandal. Bardot was so paranoid that she was supposedly convinced her phone was tapped. At the same time, their affair was so out in the open that Bardot's mother told friends that her daughter had finally found herself and come into her own now that she was with Gainsbourg.

Instead of returning to the eager arms of Gainsbourg after the filming of *Shalako* wrapped up, Brigitte Bardot went back to Gunter Sachs. Even though the whole affair lasted for only a few months, Gainsbourg was destroyed. "It's like when you break a string on a guitar, it's very dangerous. It scarred me," he said. "She left her mark, no question." He was prone to dramatically telling friends he was going to throw himself into the Seine. "I was at his side the whole time during that week when Bardot dumped him. Serge wanted to blow his brains out. He was really in love with her, but his pride was also shattered," his friend Claude Dejacques said. "Going out with her was an enormous boost to his ego because it was like he was triumphing over his own ugliness, which early on had caused him great suffering."

By then Gainsbourg was so famous as a singer, songwriter, and occasional actor that he was roughly the French equivalent of Bob Dylan, Barbra Streisand, Prince, Bruce Springsteen, and Phil Spector put together. The press loved the guessing game of whom Gainsbourg would date next. He was portrayed in the media as an unlikely ladies' man. But he also loved to demonize women as the reason his relationships ended badly. A March 4, 1968, article written by Michel Derain for *Paris Jour* quotes Gainsbourg saying, "I will never be gentle with women. I hate them. It always ends badly between us."

Such was Gainsbourg's saturnine emotional state when he met Jane Birkin while doing screen tests for *Slogan*. Birkin was also melancholy from her divorce, but was desperate to reclaim her life. Pierre Grimblat, the director, suspected that Gainsbourg was being particularly rude to his scene partner because he was simply reacting out of ego and misogyny, annoyed that this British unknown was going to be cast as his costar. But what neither man could deny was that Birkin and Gainsbourg had chemistry, and that's what the movie needed. The characters they played were two strangers already in relationships. In the screenplay, their first encounter occurs after Gainsbourg's director character wins a prize and is taking an elevator to his hotel room. He hears a dog barking and, when enough people exit, he sees the dog in the arms of a young woman with a bow in her hair wearing short shorts and carrying a woven basket. Their eye contact lingers. They are strangers to each other, but there is something beyond just anonymity between them. In a comedy that makes liberal use of broad acting, it is a genuine moment where there is a spark of real curiosity between them.

After Birkin arrived home in London, she got the call that the role was hers. But she had to wait to return to Paris. Before she and Gainsbourg could get to know each other at any great depth or even start filming, everything in France halted for a student-led revolution.

Political instability was pulsating in France, with calls for President Charles de Gaulle and his Gaullist affiliated parties, which had ruled since the end of World War II, to finally be replaced by more progressive candidates. The newspaper *Le Monde* called France bored, too apathetic to take part in the youth politics happening on campuses in Germany and in the United States. In March 1968, however, a group of students, artists, and leftists met at the University of Paris at Nanterre, a campus in the suburbs. The meeting had a wide range of topics, including discussing class and politics and how the university's funding was allocated, and occupied administration buildings. Their demands were more philosophical in comparison to the counterculture movement in the United States and what was happening on American campuses: The French students were protesting the war in Vietnam while also opposing the old guard's hold on their country. From the behavior of its politicians to the casual insults hurled against women by Gainsbourg, France was patriarchal, and progressive students were calling for a change.

Someone in the administration called the police, who surrounded the university and effectively disbanded the gathering. As a result, Nanterre was closed temporarily. A wave of student protests followed at various other Paris universities, including the Sorbonne, where students occupied an amphitheater on May 3, 1968. The police showed up with barricades and batons, beating students and arresting six hundred. The students responded with what some might call rioting and others might call a logical reaction to the overt police presence: They built their own barricades and threw stones, and the police hit them with tear gas and mass arrests.

For weeks Paris, and then all of France, was paralyzed. Strikes, protests, and riots grew larger and larger. Professors and high school students struck in solidarity; factory workers and unions all over the country walked off the job; millions of citizens participated in marches. It was a massive, national period of civil disobedience that had far-reaching consequences. Ten million workers stopped going into work, instead protesting or occupying the factories and buildings where they were normally employed. Mail wasn't being delivered, freight at shipyards wasn't getting loaded or unloaded, trains and the Paris Métro were not running, gas stations were out of fuel. Because the television system was owned by the state, there were no reports on what was happening. The Cannes Film Festival was canceled halfway through because of all the strikes and protests. And Jane Birkin certainly wasn't getting into the country to start filming a comedy.

May 1968 was a student rebellion aided by workers' protests that ushered in a new government after de Gaulle resigned in 1969. In addition to being a signal of a new generation of political action, this kicked off a cultural and sexual revolution. The students and children of what was known as "May '68" became identifiable, culturally and politically, similar to how baby boomers in America were considered the Woodstock generation. They were forever changed by a society that gradually opened up to issues like feminism and workers' rights. It also signified a broader—and belated, compared to London or the United States—embrace and exploration of youth culture that Birkin and Gainsbourg would benefit from, even if they had a flippant relationship to the idea of massive political unrest. "We didn't think about May '68," said Birkin of how she and her costar Gainsbourg regarded the disruption in filming. "He didn't take it seriously. He was Russian! It seemed anecdotal compared to the October Revolution."

In June 1968, the tension in Paris had settled enough that filming could begin. Birkin flew into Le Bourget Airport with a nanny for her daughter and checked into the Hôtel Esmeralda, a former seventeenth-century mansion on rue Saint-Julien-Le-Pauvre in the Latin Quarter, right near the English-language bookstore Shakespeare and Company and close enough to Notre-Dame to have a view of the Gothic cathedral. Her brother was also staying in the hotel. Post–*2001: A Space Odyssey*, Andrew was location-scouting for a potential Stanley Kubrick project on Napoleon. He was just a year older than his sister—twenty-two to her twenty-one in the summer of 1968—and they had always been close, but he was particularly a balm for her as she was navigating her largest film role to date, a divorce, and a baby. Andrew was sometimes tasked with watching Kate, taking her on scouting trips and photographing his young niece perched atop Napoleon's throne.

Shortly after the beginning of shooting, Birkin returned home from a day on set and complained to Andrew about Gainsbourg's unbearably large ego and how he was an ungenerous scene partner. She also found him pretentious for showing up to the set with dozens of notes on the manuscript. When he looked at her, she said, he always seemed like he was about to say something sarcastic at her expense. She found his attitude full of contempt.

After three nights of her complaining, Andrew returned to the hotel following a day spent photographing Joséphine Bonaparte's bedroom at Château de Malmaison. Birkin was on the phone with Gainsbourg, "struggling with her nemesis." Andrew was the closest person to Birkin in the world, and he had a sense that the pair needed to talk through this clash of personalities. But there was a heightened tone to her voice on the phone and a self-satisfied expression that stopped him, so much that he took out his camera to capture the moment. (His sister had been one of his primary artistic focuses since childhood; it can be argued that Birkin's first role as muse was really for Andrew.) He snapped a few photos of her on the hotel bed with its flocked headboard and matching wallpaper, cradling the big white phone receiver in her left hand. She had a hint of a smile on her face, as if animosity was not the only emotion between her and Gainsbourg. Andrew Birkin thought that, under all his sister's frustration with her costar, there was a flirtatious note to her voice as well.

Pierre Grimblat, the director, suggested to his stars that they all go to the beloved Belle Époque restaurant Maxim's for dinner to get to know each other in a less fraught environment than a film set. Grimblat left after the meal, and Gainsbourg and Birkin continued to share the evening together. He took her to Régine's, a club owned by a plump woman with a wild backstory involving orphanhood and claims that Warren Beatty, Robert Mitchum, Steve McQueen, Gene Kelly, and Françoise Sagan were all former lovers. Her Paris club had a celeb-friendly, anything-goes-for-the-beautiful-people policy such as Studio 54 would later have. Gainsbourg and Brigitte Bardot had gone there frequently during their affair because Régine had a reputation for protecting her guests from leaked gossip. And that night, Gainsbourg and Birkin found themselves under the lights there. Birkin took a turn dancing to the novelty hit "Yummy Yummy Yummy (I Got Love in My Tummy)." He asked her to dance, but wanted to wait for something slow. It turned out that Gainsbourg was not a very good dancer, which Birkin found rather delightful; the maladroitness broke through his cocky facade. She liked how awkward and shy he seemed away from the tension of the *Slogan* set. "I understood that all these things I had seen as aggression were really just defense mechanisms of someone infinitely too sensitive, terribly romantic, with a tenderness and sentimentality that no one could imagine existed," she wrote. "One day he told me that he was a 'phony villain,' which is true."

She softened to him more and more over the course of the night. They went to another club called La Calavados to watch a group of Mexican singers. Once they arrived, Gainsbourg sat at the piano and did a four-hander with the other pianist on duty. Then he and Birkin moved on to Raspoutine, a Russian nightclub Gainsbourg frequented. Everywhere they went, Gainsbourg handed out money for tips he kept in cash in a briefcase, saying, "We are all prostitutes." They ended the night at Madame Arthur, a drag cabaret, where Gainsbourg's father had once played piano and where Gainsbourg still knew many of the old-timers. She was charmed by the atmosphere. "They would shout 'Oh, hi Serge!' and shower him with kisses, the feathers from their hair sticking into my face the whole time," she wrote.

As they left, he asked musicians at the club to play Jean Sibelius's "Valse Triste" on the pavement while they headed to a Pigalle market that was opening at dawn, and Gainsbourg seemed to know everyone there as he passed around glasses of champagne he poured for workers.

By then it was morning, but Birkin didn't want the night to end. He asked her if she wanted to be dropped off back at the hotel, but she said no, surprising herself at her own candor. But she wasn't sure where they were headed. "I thought he was going to take me home to his parents, but to my horror, he brought me to the Hilton, where they said at the desk, 'Same room as usual, Mr. Gainsbourg?'"

she said. "I thought, 'Oh, no!'" John Barry was still the only person she had slept with. She wasn't looking for a drunken one-night stand with her costar. When the two of them got to the hotel room, she excused herself to go to the bathroom to buy herself time to think. When she came out, he was asleep. So she left and walked to a drugstore, where she bought a copy of "Yummy Yummy Yummy" as a souvenir of the night. She returned and carefully placed the record between Gainsbourg's toes, then went back to the Hôtel Esmeralda.

People who knew Birkin and Gainsbourg often say that their love was instant—that after that first night at Maxim's and Régine's, they were inseparable. Rather than taking time to process their various failed marriages and whether getting into another serious relationship was the most practical idea, they fell into immediate coupledom. The pair did not take things slowly despite their fresh divorces and the fact that both had small children.

Gainsbourg was eighteen years older than Birkin, an even greater age difference than the thirteen years between her and John Barry. But unlike her ex-husband, Gainsbourg was wildly energetic and wanted to spend all his time with her. He went out every night, and instead of assuming Birkin would stay home with her baby, he brought Kate along. The couple thrived on grand, romantic gestures. Early in their courtship, at eight o'clock at night, Gainsbourg turned to Birkin and told her that he loved her so much that he had asked for all the monuments in the city to be illuminated at the same time. The truth was that all the monuments lit up at eight anyway, but Birkin either fell for it or was so smitten that she found the whole ruse endearing. When she returned to London for a few days, he sent her a postcard that included the lines "The loveliest telegram / Of all the telegrams." Birkin later looked back on those early days with tenderness. Their romance had all the simple joy and lack of worry that come with being young and in love.

Meanwhile they were finishing shooting *Slogan* in Paris and Venice. Birkin and Gainsbourg no longer had friction on set; just the opposite. The movie was getting in the way of, or was just a background for, their burgeoning relationship. The couple gave off a feeling that nothing else existed outside the two of them, and it came across on the screen. Their director was a good sport, claiming in his journals that he loved them as a couple. Grimblat was also a savvy marketer—he knew that a relationship between the stars of his movie could be good fodder for promoting *Slogan* when it would be released the following year.

Birkin sensed that she should get her brother acquainted with her new love, and she invited Andrew to join her and Gainsbourg for dinner. She was relieved that the two men took an instant shine to each other. "For my part, it was love at first sight," Andrew recalled. "Serge was so utterly different from anyone I'd ever met: shy and flamboyant by turns, with a boy-like lust for fun and a scabrous sense of humor. I'd already had several mentors, not least Stanley Kubrick, but unique among them, Serge treated me as an equal. He could speak little English and my French was no better than Jane's, yet we managed to have a lively debate about Napoleon, communism, and the student riots."

Jane Birkin was relieved not only that she had his stamp of approval, but that it could help establish a family dynamic. Gainsbourg's son Paul was just a few months old when he and Birkin met; Kate Barry was a year old. Accounts of how much Gainsbourg wanted to be involved with his two eldest children vary, but he appeared to be largely absent from their lives. Instead, he was Kate Barry's stand-in *papa*, as John Barry was absent from her life. But the truth was, Gainsbourg and Birkin spent most of their free time while not filming either out in Paris together or locked up in a bedroom. The role of day-to-day father figure was occupied cheerfully by Andrew Birkin.

Judy Campbell remembered the first time she heard about Birkin and Gainsbourg as a couple: "My daughter came home and declared: 'I have to tell you something. You know that horrible Frenchman I told you about? Well I think I'm in love with him. I believe he loves me, too.'" Birkin worried that her parents might not approve of this older man, but she didn't need to. They were relieved that she was recovering from the shambles of her marriage to John Barry. Her mother thought Gainsbourg looked like Eric Maschwitz, who had written a song for her once (a narcissistic reason to like someone if ever there was one—not to mention that the two men looked nothing alike), and her father thought he was hilarious. John Barry had never cared about nurturing a strong relationship with Birkin's parents, particularly following the negotiation about when she was allowed to get married. But they got along well with Serge, who loved big gestures, such as giving Cartier bracelets to Campbell. And Birkin found Gainsbourg's family to be warm and old-world in their manners. All of it felt like this relationship was marking the end of her turbulent adolescent years.

The relationship benefited Gainsbourg as well. Like Birkin, he was a romantic who fell in love easily and hard. Birkin was different from the French women he had been coupled with: goofy, eccentric, full of excitement. But there were other perks to dating her. He did not have much subcultural capital; he was always mainstream, a hitmaker. He was a forty-year-old who could be aging out of relevance at any time, particularly in the new Parisian cultural scene post–May '68. Having a gorgeous, extremely young girl from London on his arm gave him some cachet. Birkin was such an unknown in France that no one was reporting on her yet. Their own jet-set coterie saw them out in the clubs or at Brasserie Lipp having dinner and were well aware that Gainsbourg had rebounded from his affair with Brigitte Bardot with John Barry's ex, who had been in the edgy hit *Blow-Up*. But neither paparazzo photographers nor the tabloid press had discovered them by mid-1968.

In August 1968, Gainsbourg and Birkin moved into L'Hôtel on rue des Beaux-Arts, a neighborhood hostelry with just twenty rooms where Oscar Wilde had lived out his last days before his death. It was a bit like the Chelsea Hotel of Paris: Frank Sinatra, Grace Kelly, Salvador Dalí, and another infamously dramatic couple, Richard Burton and Elizabeth Taylor, had all stayed there, and Jim Morrison would check in a couple years later, in the early '70s. Unlike the Chelsea, it was not a place of artistic collaboration, but somewhere for Birkin and Gainsbourg to isolate themselves. A tiny hotel was the perfect spot to block out the world in the way that new love invites.

Their physical attraction was electric. Birkin was his type, more so than Bardot had been. Gainsbourg had drawn girls like her when he was an art student, and took her to the Louvre to show her paintings by the German Renaissance-era artist Lucas Cranach the Elder. He said that she was a Cranach, with tiny breasts, a small waist, and narrow hips. After being teased for her body at boarding school, singing comedic songs about increasing her bust when she was cast in *Passion Flower Hotel* in the West End, and enduring the betrayal of John Barry, she felt beautiful, even erotic, in his gaze. And while the never-ending remark about how ugly Gainsbourg was pervaded the culture, she found him deeply sexy. Birkin later joked that people could "recognise us from the back because of my basket and his ears." She didn't mean so unkindly; she preferred the kind of man who wrote or read under an umbrella on the beach rather than one who was flexing his muscles. And she loved Gainsbourg's face. "When you've known a face like that, others seem bland," she said.

It was the first time Birkin felt real intimacy with a man, both emotionally and physically. That ease allowed her to go outside of her comfort zone—not to somehow impress her new lover but to test out her own desires. Birkin and Gainsbourg took to egging each other on in a game of erotic one-upmanship as she came into a newfound confidence in her sexuality. Gainsbourg loved to ask Birkin, "What have you never done?" Birkin asked Gainsbourg to take her to a sex hotel. Her fantasy was to go to the most sordid and decrepit one that they could find and ask for a room for her to playact as a sex worker. They found one in Pigalle, in Paris's red-light district, near where Gainsbourg had grown up. She and Gainsbourg drank two cognacs to work up the nerve before asking the man at the front desk for a room. The man asked how old Birkin was, referring to her as "the little one." Gainsbourg said she was of age—which was true; she was in her early twenties, and the age of sexual maturity in France, *la majorité sexuelle*, was set at fifteen years old—and after some discerning looks, they were handed a key. Off they went to their dingy room. It was overly brightly lit, with plastic flowers as décor, a bed that was damp, and a bidet with a tap that dripped. Before they could decide if the fantasy even turned them on anymore, the door to the room was broken down by four men who were convinced Birkin was underage and being taken advantage of.

She and Gainsbourg were shaken and left for home. In their upscale hotel in the bourgeois Left Bank neighborhood, no one noticed, was suspicious, or cared about what they were up to.

That summer, Birkin sent her friend Gabrielle Crawford a postcard that read, "I have fallen madly in love. John no longer exists." Much of the initial connection between Birkin and Gainsbourg was based on finding a sense of belonging within each other. He was much more up front about his emotions than John; he was unafraid to cry, and Birkin connected to that sensitivity. But another, perhaps more intangible side of their relationship was that he represented Paris, and Paris was part of the allure of her new life: stopping to browse the used-book stalls that lined the river, sitting outside drinking wine with friends without much caring about the time. She'd go to Maxim's and steal plates and silverware as souvenirs by hiding them in her underwear. Nothing felt like it had real consequences. The city seemed to have innumerable secrets that revealed themselves to her the more she explored, like how she could go into the catacombs under the streets and find herself coming up by the Eiffel Tower. Gainsbourg took her to dinner parties at Régine's apartment, where the cultural minister and novelist André Malraux would be discussing ghosts with the *Bonjour tristesse* novelist Françoise Sagan and a newspaper gossip columnist. She was falling in love with Gainsbourg at the same time she was falling in love with a city. Birkin delighted in it all; Paris and its people and her new boyfriend were all intertwined in a heady mix of pleasure and relief from a rough beginning to her adult years. London might have been a cultural center, but she was having more fun in Paris, where falling in love in the aftermath of May '68 gave their relationship an extra element of urgency.

The year 1968 had not just changed France; it had changed both Birkin and Gainsbourg. She'd spent the early months of 1968 in a miserable marriage while Gainsbourg was still brooding over Brigitte Bardot. They met in May 1968, fell in love in the weeks following, and were living together by August. Birkin thrilled to the expedited pace of it all; she was living in the moment. Decades later, she said, "I left for France with my daughter and got a part in *Slogan* with Serge Gainsbourg, and fell in love with him. I didn't really have time to think. I had no great ambition. Ambition came later."

Claiming she didn't have ambition was not exactly true. Birkin was certainly living in the moment, like so many people of her generation were in a time when daily life seemed on the precipice of revolution. But the ambition was always there. She didn't just want to be Gainsbourg's girlfriend; she wanted to work.

CHAPTER FOUR

It's Like She's Not Acting at All

Jane Birkin decided she would go back to London after shooting for *Slogan* wrapped in August 1968. She was conscious of the dependent dynamic she'd had with her ex John Barry and didn't want to fall back into it with new beau Serge Gainsbourg. His reaction to the prospect of her leaving was to quietly cry in front of a candle all night—"very Russian, very dramatic," she wrote in her journal, sounding exasperated and flattered at the same time.

On what was supposed to be Birkin's last night in Paris, she had dinner with *Slogan*'s director. Despite the rocky beginning of the shoot, Pierre Grimblat was happy with the film and thought Birkin had a lot of promise. He told another director, Jacques Deray, that he should consider Birkin for his next movie, *La piscine* (*The Swimming Pool*), which was to start shooting in a few months in the South of France. Deray came to the restaurant that night to spy on her, and *voilà*, charmed by her presence, he later offered her the part. It was a major turning point for Birkin. Instead of returning to her home country to try out independence, Birkin made the decision to choose her career, choose France, and choose Gainsbourg.

La piscine is a psychological thriller about two lovers vacationing at a house with a large pool outside Saint-Tropez in the South of France. The male half of the couple is Jean-Paul, played by the French movie star and heartthrob Alain Delon, known for his piercing blue eyes, high cheekbones, and air of danger. Delon was more pretty—almost too pretty—than handsome, and his screen persona often centered on cold antihero characters, like the hit man he played in the 1967 film *Le samouraï*, directed by Jean-Pierre Melville, or René Clément's *Purple Noon*, which was based on Patricia Highsmith's novel *The Talented Mr. Ripley*. To add an additional layer of dramatic tension, Jean-Paul's lover in the film, Marianne, was played by the Vienna-born actress Romy Schneider, who was the real-life ex of Delon. She had come to fame as a teen playing Sissi, the nineteenth-century empress of Austria, in a series of movies.

In the film, Jean-Paul and Marianne's blissfully lazy days of swimming, making out, and eating breakfast in bed are interrupted by the arrival of Marianne's former paramour and Jean-Paul's former best friend Harry (played by Maurice Ronet) and Harry's eighteen-year-old daughter, Penelope (played by Birkin). Penelope had been raised by her mother in the UK, and Harry had just recently learned of her existence and was eager to get to know her. Early on, the focus of the film seems to be on the love triangle between Marianne, Harry, and Jean-Paul, exploring themes of resentment, friendship, sex, and jealousy among people in their thirties and forties. Birkin's Penelope is often seen relegated to the background, wandering around or lounging silently by the pool as the tension between the adults slowly ratchets up. Her character is supposed to be about two decades younger than everyone else; as a result, Birkin was costumed in her own clothes and did her own makeup. In her first scene, getting out of the car with a father she barely knows, she wears a white button-up shirt tucked into a gray miniskirt, black ballet flats, and giant, round sunglasses with baby-blue lenses. While Marianne swans around her home wearing oversize men's shirts and caftans, Penelope skulks about awkwardly dressed like she came directly from school rather than for a vacation by the sea. Harry, her father, watches Jean-Paul leering at her and notes, "She looks much older than she is"—which is ironic because she looks like she's about fifteen or sixteen, not even the eighteen she's supposed to be playing.

As the film goes on, Penelope's role becomes more integral to the plot. What starts as flirting by the pool with Delon's character Jean-Paul ends up with her having some kind of dalliance with him. It's not shown onscreen—the audience sees the two returning late for dinner from a long day at the beach, while Marianne and Harry can intuit what had transpired. "The first swim of the year always tires you out," Marianne says to a wide-eyed Penelope, referring to losing her virginity. As the plot twists on, Penelope starts to look more at home among the trio of adults. She doesn't try to copy the style of Marianne or look older than her eighteen years, but she's gained some experience in the world, and that sliver of confidence is reflected in her wardrobe: a blue gingham dress with a dropped waist, a white bikini, and, after her father dies, a black dress with long sleeves and an extremely short hem for his funeral.

La piscine is not a film that aspires to be talky, nor is it madcap or even a traditional psychological thriller. There is seemingly not a lot going on for long stretches beyond mood and atmosphere. The vibe is as day-drunk and woozy in the dry heat as the characters for whom a trip into town to buy groceries for dinner is a big event. Birkin's Penelope is similarly not doing a lot. But what Harry and Jean-Paul and Marianne experience mirrors the same feeling the audience of the movie has, which is to be stunned just by Birkin's onscreen presence. She's so awkward in an adolescent way and petulant in her manner that she comes across as a spectral figure. Her wide-set eyes and gap teeth and slim body only add to her preternatural being. What exactly Birkin is doing so well comes across so effortlessly, it's like she's not performing at all.

The actual range of Birkin's acting in *La piscine* can be understood only when you consider her own backstory. She was playing a schoolgirl and a virgin who was so convincing in her lack of guile that it is easy for viewers of the film to assume Birkin was simply playing herself. The reality was that Birkin in 1968 was already a divorcée and a mother at twenty-one. She had seen and experienced life in a way that her character Penelope had not. She was acting, but her style was so naturalistic that she performed the trick of not seeming like she was doing much at all.

Director Jacques Deray wanted to keep up the ruse that she was just an innocent former schoolgirl for the film's shooting and release. Birkin noticed that Schneider brought her son David to play with Delon's son Anthony on the set, so she followed suit and brought

Kate. Deray screamed at her for bringing her daughter, potentially ruining the image of her as an eighteen-year-old identical to Penelope. She took Kate and locked herself in the bathroom and refused to come out until Deray apologized. Why anyone on set or in the press would need to think she was a teenage virgin to promote the film is unclear, particularly since her relationship with John Barry was, if not well-known in France, certainly not a secret.

The set had its fair share of tension, generally. Birkin's lack of mastery of the French language became a problem: Even though Deray knew she had filmed just one French movie and had lived in the country for less than a year, he was frustrated with her diction. The director tried to get her to practice speaking with a pencil in her mouth so she'd articulate better in the film. She took to learning French off a tape recorder and parroting whatever slang Gainsbourg thought she should know.

Despite these stresses, this was the first film in which Birkin took an interest in the technical aspects of filmmaking. Knowing the crew and understanding what they did were important to her, and would remain so for the rest of her life as an actor. She befriended them easily on *La piscine*, going out with them on Friday nights to eat *tarte tropézienne*, the region's signature cake layered with pastry cream. She also was savvy enough to recognize that the crew's loyalty could help her performance. She noticed the focus puller was always measuring the distance between the camera and Alain Delon's face with a measuring tape. One day she asked why and he replied, "Follow the money," meaning that the star needed to be perfectly in focus.

The movie was a box office success in France and critically acclaimed worldwide for its atmospheric erotic languor. Birkin wanted to be like her costars Alain Delon and Romy Schneider, who were not only some of the most attractive people of the twentieth century but also regarded as more than simply pretty faces. They were lauded and serious European actors, seen as real artists. Penelope was Birkin's breakout role, one in which she wasn't the comedic foil as in *Slogan* or a sexy teen as in *Blow-Up*. The cast was praised as an ensemble. In her diaries, she undervalued her own role in *La piscine*'s success: "I felt like a child who had been granted permission to play with the grown-ups, not really comprehending the importance of my own part, just carried along by the others." Nearly fifty years later she remained just as hard on herself. She told the *Guardian* in 2017 that when she looked back at her early roles in *Blow-Up* or *La piscine*, she was unimpressed and found her acting uninteresting.

During the filming, Birkin and Gainsbourg rented a house near the set. Oumède, the area where they shot *La piscine*, was full of private lanes and rambling villas, just a few miles away from the crowds and the docked yachts of Saint-Tropez. The region was lush, with lilies and laurel, palms and papyrus, groves of olive trees and vineyards that met the sea. The way the environment of the South of France was captured in such detail is part of the lasting allure of the film. Compared to Paris, Oumède was much hotter, drier, and slower.

As idyllic as that area was, Gainsbourg and Birkin would come to prefer the more austere beaches on France's Atlantic coast in Normandy or Brittany for their country living. The South of France did not represent pure freedom for them, as it was Brigitte Bardot's home territory. In fact, they ran into her in town at one point during a night out in Saint-Tropez. Birkin saw Gainbourg's face turn pale. Instead of having any kind of mature reaction to the situation, he went right for the piano and started the theme song to James Bond, which had been composed by Birkin's ex-husband, John Barry. The truth was that all three were just as insecure about one another as the trio of lead characters were in *La piscine*. As happy as he was with Birkin, Gainsbourg was still dealing with the blow to his ego of Bardot leaving him eight months before. Birkin thought he needed to be nurtured, but Bardot also brought out her own insecurities about her body. She considered herself the opposite of Brigitte Bardot, who embodied the *vedette*, a term for star, and a sultry one at that. "She inspired jealousy, whereas I inspired friendliness," Birkin said. "I wasn't dangerous; women didn't have the impression I was going to steal their husbands." Bardot remained quiet on what she thought of Birkin and Gainsbourg's relationship (although for years Birkin would donate money at the end of the year to Bardot's animal charity, and Bardot would handwrite a thank-you note back).

Gainsbourg was also contending with his own territorial feelings about Birkin. While she filmed *La piscine*, he spent his days drinking rosé, playing *pétanque* (the region's omnipresent lawn bowling game, at which he was quite poor), and carrying around a gun, which he claimed he would use on anyone who dared make eyes at Birkin, including Alain Delon. He was paranoid that another film set could mean another affair and hired a chauffeur-driven Rolls-Royce to pick her up each evening after filming, less as a way to ease exhaustion from the shoot than to make sure she was coming straight home to him. He wanted to isolate her; privately, she found his antics exhausting enough that she second-guessed her choice to be with him. After filming *La piscine*, back in Paris in the fall of 1968, she admits in her diary that she became involved in this relationship too quickly: "Now he loves me and in a way I want that and I love him, and I also want the world because, through him, I began again."

Just as Birkin's professional ambition was starting to take shape, she chose to double down on her relationship with Gainsbourg. They were quite publicly in love, but despite Birkin's gushing devotion she had moments of doubt, even in these heady first few months of her time with Gainsbourg. She might have expressed the push and pull she felt between independence and dependence only in her journal, but there was some small part of her that intuited she might be losing herself to another older, emotionally volatile man. However, there was no time to sort out those feelings because she and Gainsbourg were ready to move on from being costars to collaborating in a different medium: music.

CHAPTER FIVE

"Je t'aime . . . moi non plus"

Jane Birkin's foray into pop music, via an artistic collaboration with Serge Gainsbourg, was not entirely her idea. He had written a song for Brigitte Bardot during their brief fling in late 1967 after Bardot demanded he write her the most beautiful love song he could conceive of. It was called "Je t'aime . . . moi non plus." ("I Love You, Me Neither" is the literal translation, but one that makes more sense in English is "I Love You, Neither Do I.") They had even recorded a demo version of it in Paris that the press got their hands on. *France Dimanche*, the Sunday paper, reported that the "groans, sighs, and Bardot's little cries of pleasure [give] the impression you're listening to two people making love." Bardot's husband at the time, Gunter Sachs, also heard about the song. He gave Bardot an ultimatum to choose between him and Gainsbourg. After their affair ended, Bardot wrote Gainsbourg a letter asking him not to release "Je t'aime . . . moi non plus," so it was shelved. But he still thought it was one of the strongest he had ever written and wanted to rerecord it with a new girl.

He suggested that Birkin sing it, but she refused, citing Bardot's version as impossible to re-create. So Gainsbourg got to work finding someone else to record it. Whether he was trying reverse psychology or really just wanted to find another duet partner, it worked. Birkin heard rumors that Marianne Faithfull, the actress Valérie Lagrange, and Alain Delon's paramour Mireille Darc were all considering it. In her diary, Birkin pictured Darc wearing a kilt and lying on the sofa, asking, "So, Sergio, what has become of that little song?" and that image was enough to change her mind. His ploy worked; Birkin had worked herself up to enough jealousy that she agreed to do it.

Birkin's singing experience was limited. She sang alone in the bath, and she had sung the theme song to *Slogan*. Her role in *Passion Flower Hotel* in London showcased a certain vocal spunkiness, but that was musical comedy. The truth was that her voice was not exceptional; it was high-pitched, a little reedy, and prone to going off-key. But she was able to fully infuse songs with a sense of character and personality. "I was the figure of fun in the musical, and they used my flat chest and bandy legs as the fun image. I did have a little song, but it wasn't until 'Je t'aime . . . moi non plus' that somebody thought I had a pretty voice," she said.

"Je t'aime . . . moi non plus" was laden with sexual innuendo that crossed over into abundant and direct horniness. The song was slow and talky, unfolding like two lovers whispering to each other in bed. There were references to thrusting, coming and going, and carnality in Gainsbourg's part of the duet; meanwhile, Birkin's singing consisted of mostly whimpering as she cooed "I love you, I love you, Oh God, I love you" in the song's *pièce de résistance*. They recorded the song in London, in a studio in Piccadilly, in just two takes, with Gainsbourg taking special attention to conduct the "Oh God, I love you" part as an orchestra of moans, even telling Birkin to cool off on the heavy breathing at one point—that it was a little too much. Birkin's vocals were recorded in such an authentically orgasmic way that rumors would later abound that they were actually having sex while recording it. The engineer, William Flageollet, claimed to have witnessed groping, but Birkin and Gainsbourg groped in public, and often. Birkin thought that rumor was funny, albeit incorrect.

After recording, they took the ferry from London back home to Paris for the holidays in late 1968. Upon arrival, they went out to dinner at one of their regular spots at the Hôtel des Beaux Arts. There happened to be a record player in the room. Gainsbourg walked over and, without announcing his intentions, put on "Je t'aime . . . moi non plus." Everyone stopped talking, their knives and forks suspended in midair as they listened to the coos and the lyrics about loins. He nudged Birkin and said, "I think we've got a hit record."

"Je t'aime . . . moi non plus" came out in February 1969 and immediately became the number one song in France, staying on the charts for eighteen months. Gainsbourg had been famous in France, but this was his first truly worldwide hit song. It charted at number one in England. "Je t'aime . . . moi non plus" debuted in the United States at number eighty-nine, at which point Birkin and Gainsbourg flew to America to do press: *Playboy*, *Merv Griffin*, *Dick Cavett*. The audiences there didn't know her yet, so she was occasionally introduced as the girl from the film *Blow-Up*. Worldwide, the single eventually sold more than six million copies.

They released a kind of proto–music video for it, selling the idea of languid Parisian sultriness: holding each other under the Eiffel Tower; making sly eye contact, looking like they were enjoying a private joke. The chemistry between them was electric. Birkin was immediately met with curiosity and fanfare on a global stage, outpacing any coverage she'd had in her years acting in London. Her image became inescapable in the media that year, and she was graduating into real international stardom. But her fame was tied to Gainsbourg. She was the woman whose girlish singing had propelled his song to become a worldwide hit; she was the one the French troubadour was in love with. *Jours de France* had a shot of her face on its cover with an article titled "At 21, Jane Birkin Has All the Luck," including photos of her wearing a fluffy fur coat with a miniskirt, beaming at Gainsbourg, and another carrying Kate on her hip. Another *Jours de France* cover had Birkin kissing Kate on the nose. "The Englishwoman Who Was Conquered by Paris but Who Conquered Serge Gainsbourg" was splashed across *La vie Parisienne.* "World Famous in Three Minutes" was the title of the article about her in the Swiss magazine *Schweizer Illustrierte*. In Spain, *Siete Dias Ilustrados* titled a story about her "The Bored Gazelle"; "Jane Proves the Language of Love Is Universal," wrote the British music paper *Melody Maker*. A BBC report on Birkin and Gainsbourg after the release of "Je t'aime . . . moi non plus" described a glittering party in Paris attended by Madame Georges Pompidou, the wife of the president; the younger fashion crowd; and eighteen helmeted officers of the French household cavalry. "But the girl who got the most eyes at her entrance wasn't even French at all. She's twenty-three-year-old Jane Birkin, and English to the eyebrows," a newscaster narrated over footage of Birkin peering under her long bangs, laughing. "Open any magazine in Paris and you'll find her somewhere inside. . . . It's a storybook success saga all the more exotic in that it's happened in another country."

"Je t'aime . . . moi non plus" was met with plenty of censorship. The BBC banned it; the head of Phonogram Records, Gainsbourg and Birkin's Italian label, was thrown into jail for it; in South America, the record was slipped into sleeves of a Maria Callas record in order to be sold. The Vatican denounced the song, which made it seem even more titillating. ("The pope has been our best publicist," Birkin later said.) "Erotic Record Shunned," wrote *Melody Maker* in the August 23, 1969, issue. The German magazine *Pop* had a photo of Birkin looking especially wan, eyes looking down with the word *verboten* in red across the cover. "Jane and I have this in common: We like to scandalize the world" was the pull quote in the Belgian paper *Le Soir Illustré.* Birkin had not anticipated so much frenzy around the song or the level of fame it immediately brought her, but she enjoyed the spotlight as half of the most provocative couple in pop.

Gainsbourg said impishly that it was the most moral song he had ever written. Birkin was equally faux naïve, or at least tinged by the all-consuming love affair she was in the middle of. She thought the song was romantic rather than pornographic. "It wasn't a rude song at all. I don't know what all the fuss was about," she said in 2004. "I'm still not sure they know what it means." All the backlash helped turn the single into a *succès de scandale*, something people, particularly young people, could listen to in secret and feel rebellious for enjoying.

During this massive wave of notoriety, they already had another project ready to go. After Georges Meyerstein-Maigret, the head of Philips, their record label, heard the recording of "Je t'aime . . . moi non plus" at the end of 1968, he'd asked them to return to London in January 1969 to complete a whole album. He recognized that the overt sexuality and inevitable controversy would be an uphill battle, but he was willing to risk it, joking that he was willing to go to prison, but for an album, not a single.

Gainsbourg was the songwriter for the album, but Birkin and their relationship provided the inspiration. France's most lauded troubadour had debuted his latest muse. Gainsbourg's role was defined and active, but the role of muse was regarded as much more passive. It was her personality and her love for him that had drawn such career heights out of him. This was the first time the public had seen Birkin in this manner—and the first time most fans beyond close watchers of *Blow-Up* or *The Knack . . . and How to Get It* had been introduced to her at all.

A full-length album proved that the sexy, dreamlike quality of Birkin's vocals and Gainsbourg's songwriting on "Je t'aime . . . moi non plus" was not the stuff of a one-hit wonder. Gainsbourg wrote "Jane B." after hearing his girlfriend singing in the bath one day. The song shared Birkin's name but was based on Vladimir Nabokov's novel *Lolita*, a lifelong obsession of Gainsbourg's. The lyrics compare and contrast *Lolita*'s adolescent protagonist Dolores Haze, with her brown hair and age of "five thousand three hundred days," to Birkin's blue eyes and age of "twenty, maybe twenty-one." Meanwhile, the song "Orang-outang" was about Birkin's precious stuffed Munkey. Inspired by the ferry the two had taken from Paris to London, "69 année érotique" sketched a fantasy in which he and his lover would take a ferry from their bed on a journey that would take a whole year and triumph over evil. Birkin's perfectly imperfect vocals elevated the songs from Gainsbourg's rambling, wordy French into pop perfection. Her voice telegraphed so much at once: sexiness and naïveté, innocence and experience. Gainsbourg and Birkin sounded more like teenagers going through their first sexual awakenings than two adults with kids and divorces. That also might be why their music was so popular and enduring: Pop music is at its best when making everyone feel like adolescents going through big feelings, no matter their age or life experience.

Duetting on an album gave the couple a new level of acclaim and visibility. The press started covering them as a couple, a kind of modern Beauty and the Beast. The media was fascinated by the pair and their perceived differences: Birkin, beautiful and young and inexperienced; Gainsbourg, a brilliant and seasoned performer who took her under his wing. Their most famous tabloid cover was an English paper called *Weekend* in April 1970 with a photo of Birkin in white bell-bottoms and a white T-shirt tied just under her breasts. She sits on Gainsbourg's lap, looking down at his face. The headline reads: "The Ugly Man I Love."

The success of the song, along with her burgeoning film career and her relationship to Gainsbourg, cemented Birkin to France. It was where she found herself. "My true liberation," she said. "Suddenly I felt accepted as an original." Even if she felt at home in France, the media persisted in presenting her as carefree and unserious. By the time she was twenty-two, Birkin had played pouty, sexually charged free spirits in *Blow-Up*, *Slogan*, and *La piscine*, solidifying her status as a go-to for the role of a wide-eyed ingénue. French interviewers would make her pronounce words like "*terrible*" with her strong accent. She was game and played along and laughed politely. In an interview for *Slogan* she did alongside Gainsbourg, the interviewer comments that watching *Slogan* feels like watching her real life. She looks slightly stricken at the statement, running her hand through her hair. She doesn't get a chance to respond—it was a comment, not a question—and the interviewer moves on to asking Gainsbourg how he felt about his role. A BBC television segment described her career in accurate but patronizing terms: "Her roles have a certain similarity, usually that of a slightly clumsy, slightly lost English girl who gets caught up in the underworld. It's the sort of part that petite little French girls wouldn't even try." Stardom was coming for Birkin so fast that she did not have time to consider the effect of these interviews on her public image at the crest of her fame. She was pretty and radiated a breezy quality that worked against her. Her image as a free-spirited ditzy girl was already starting to firm up.

At twenty-three, she gave a joint interview with Gainsbourg for the French talk show *Variances*. "I prefer this," she says, making a rolling motion with her hands like the tracks of a roller coaster, with sounds of mounting and descending to go along with it, "all the time. It's better that way. Because just that . . ." She makes a flat motion with her hands, then trails off. "He's very hard to live with." She makes this difficulty sound perfectly nonchalant, like it is all part of her carefree life. In this interview, Birkin was reckoning—if only glancingly—with the fact of her rather imbalanced relationship with Gainsbourg. But it took more time for her to unpack that—and even longer for the public to accept it.

CHAPTER SIX

Nonchalance Personified

Jane Birkin wore a white lace macramé gown to a gala at the Cannes Film Festival in May 1969. The front dipped so low it trailed past her navel; she used a black beaded brooch to keep it closed. She had intentionally worn the dress backward for the dramatic impact of a plunging neckline. She swore she wasn't trying to shock. "When you're in the middle of it, you're not thinking you're doing something shocking. If the macramé dress didn't please me because it was too high in the front, then I put it the other way around," she told the British edition of *Harper's Bazaar* in an interview with the designer Jean Paul Gaultier.

Part of being half of one of the most famous couples in the world meant that the casually brazen way Jane Birkin dressed became part of the notoriety of her relationship. To the premiere of *Slogan*, at the end of August in 1969, she wore a black jersey long-sleeved dress that fell to about two inches below her crotch. That dress was also transparent, so her lack of a bra was on full display. The rest of the outfit also inspired breathless commentary: bikini underwear, two long gold chains, and Mary Janes, a basket bag in one hand and the other arm intertwined with Gainsbourg's. She claimed for the rest of her life that she had no idea the dress would be see-through, but, regardless of her intentions, it solidified her reputation as a fashion risk-taker.

Birkin's look was nonchalance personified. She became an easy entry point for the fashion press to cover countercultural styles because she was beautiful and famous and, more than that, actually lived a bohemian lifestyle. She was daring in style but she was also palatable. She wasn't a hippie but rather a rising star from the upper class—she had an imprimatur. Yet it was fresh enough to help establish her as a symbol of the generational divide.

Ciné Revue in 1969 called her style "The Emancipated Venus of the New Age" in a spread of photos showing her in cropped cotton tops and barely there beaded shirts, taken at parties with Gainsbourg or on the street. Her image was seemingly enough; there was no accompanying interview. *Petticoat* magazine ran her makeup routine in 1968 ("No lipstick. Just a brown pencil outline on the top"). *Pariscope* devoted a whole story to "Jane's Basket" in the early '70s, detailing the maps, cigarettes, daily planner, and single red-and-white-striped woolen sock that were found inside. The basket had been her signature since she lived in London, and it always caused a scene. She claimed she was once denied entry to the restaurant Maxim's because of it. She refused to ditch it, and Gainsbourg made a scene outside the restaurant, yelling, "If you don't let her in the way she is, we're going." It wasn't just about refusing norms; the bag, the aesthetic, the barefaced makeup, were all about Birkin projecting a confidence and an ease of self that brought together many of the dominant looks of the time while also transcending any single trend. It was a look wholly unique.

Birkin's signature aesthetic really started to shine at the tail end of the 1960s. Crochet dresses, espadrilles, tiny white T-shirts, cutoff jeans, miniskirts, never a bra in sight. When done well, personal style looks like it was created sui generis by its wearer; the truth is that it's often more of a collection of references and biography. Birkin's espadrilles were a souvenir of vacations in Spain and the South of France. The forgoing of a bra was a nod to her body type. She didn't really need the support of one, physically speaking, so why wear one if she didn't want to? Of course, rejecting a layer between one's skin and clothes was about being outré and showing off a brazen sexuality, but it was also about freedom. Choosing a miniskirt over a pencil skirt, too, was about comfort—the former was easier to walk in. The rejection of high-heeled pumps was similarly about embracing boots or flat shoes as better for being on the go. Birkin was representative of her baby boom generation's desire to escape the confines of previous decades: the bullet bras, corsetry, crinolines. No more slips, unless worn as a dress.

Paris may have always been the global capital of fashion, but in terms of youth culture driving fashion, the city lagged behind the aggressively modern outfits in London and the hippies of the United States. Birkin's style stood out in contrast to the quintessential French women of the time, who looked controlled and thoroughly appropriate at all events in leopard coats, hosiery, high heels, and tailored silk suits. Birkin knew that bourgeois look wasn't her, but French women looked so well put together, so polished in comparison to her, that it managed to make her feel occasionally insecure. Womanhood, in France, was considered an art form: a tension between showing elegance, chicness, even a little coldness, merging and bumping up against seduction, provocation, and naughtiness. But after 1968 even France embraced a shift in how fashionable women dressed, led by Birkin and women who counted themselves among Yves Saint Laurent's inner circle of longtime friends-employees-muses like Loulou de la Falaise, Talitha Getty, and Betty Catroux.

The 1960s were a period of crisis for haute couture. Couture was art, but it was also associated with a world gone by. The legendary couturier Cristóbal Balenciaga closed his house in May 1968 amid the workers' protests with several parting words of outrage and ennui, including "The life of a couturier is the life of a dog" and "I will not prostitute my art." He supposedly told one client, "Why do you want me to carry on? There is no one left for me to dress." While there were still some matrons or socialites willing to buy couture from the old guard of designers—Gloria Vanderbilt, Brooke Astor, any of Truman Capote's coterie of Swans—younger women like Birkin with the means to buy designer clothes wanted less pomp, less fuss. That meant ready-to-wear, which was already dominant in London. For a new generation of designers and brands such as Pierre Cardin, André Courrèges, Paco Rabanne, Yves Saint Laurent, Thea Porter, Azzaro, Ossie Clark, Cacharel, Biba, and Emanuel Ungaro, it was time to come into their own. They were reflecting not just the bohemian trends, but also utopian and space age themes. Birkin might have been dressing for nights out at Régine's more than for revolution, but those were the designers she championed. "I don't care much about expensive couture clothes. I like the floppy look of Saint Laurent," she told *Women's Wear Daily* in 1969. Saint Laurent's designs helped define how a grown-up woman with money might embrace the changing times and counterculture with dresses that resembled Mondrian paintings, tunics inspired by safari jackets and his childhood growing up in a French family in Algeria, and tuxedos for women.

Birkin quickly became a staple in all the fashion magazines: *Vogue*, *Elle*, *Marie Claire*. She was so popular in France that she appeared on the cover of French *Vogue* at least once a year, proof that, ever since "Je t'aime . . . moi non plus" came out as a single in February 1969, she was already one of the country's biggest celebrities. Her first *Vogue* cover in May 1969 featured her wearing Cerruti and modeling jersey fabrics with her hair curled into ringlets—softer and less overtly erotic than how she dressed in real life. She understood that she didn't always have to be shot looking like herself and likened modeling to collaborating with directors. She loved the satisfaction she got at the end of a shoot when a photographer said, "I think I've got it." She was on the cover again less than a year later in March 1970 for a cheeky shoot of her in long wool coats or an ensemble of a vest with balloon-like pants stuffed into tall boots, posing in each photo next to a classical statue of a naked man with a large fig leaf over his genitalia.

With her rising global stardom, appearances in magazines outside France and England followed. In March 1969, Birkin appeared in American *Vogue* modeling the latest Yves Saint Laurent designs alongside Betty Catroux. Birkin posed wearing a black jumpsuit, paisley flares, a raincoat, and a beige shirtdress. She looked at ease, as if she just happened to be photographed in her own clothes. In the accompanying article, she was called a *femme-enfant*, a woman-child, still not allowed to be just an adult woman (let alone portrayed as a mother). A few months later, she was on the cover of

American *Vogue* for the January 1970 issue in a tight shot of her face wearing soft makeup—some blush, some mascara, a little nude lipstick—and a lilac shirt, albeit without a big written profile of her accompanying the cover. In the June 1970 issue of American *Vogue* she was shot by Bert Stern modeling midi skirts. It was part of the fashion evolution toward longer hemlines, with Birkin seen as the vanguard. Serge Gainsbourg also appeared in the spread, but more as a glorified accessory. The text alongside them read: "Jane Birkin—the girl with the cat-green eyes and swishing hair. Young and happy . . . this year's girl. Laughing it up here with her best beau, Serge Gainsbourg. Both of them white-hot stars, hitting first in Europe, blazing now on college campuses across the country with their super first album, *Je t'aime*."

Gainsbourg loved the attention her style brought them as a couple. The two would go to the Yves Saint Laurent atelier together. He would sit in "the boyfriend chair," the kind at boutiques and studios where men can sit and relax while women attend to their duties of adornment. But Gainsbourg was an active participant, smoking, watching Birkin do a little runway show, and then helping choose what to take home.

They both enjoyed making a splash in their outfits and their entrances. The pair attended the Proust Ball in December 1971, celebrating the birth centenary of the author of *À la recherche du temps perdu*. It was one of the most lavish parties of the decade for the upper echelons of European society, hosted by Baroness Marie-Hélène de Rothschild (née Baroness Marie-Hélène Naila Stephanie Josina van Zuylen van Nyevelt van de Haar) and her husband Guy de Rothschild (who was also her third cousin and head of de Rothschild Frères bank) at the nineteenth-century Château de Ferrières, about an hour east of Paris. There were 350 guests, including Elizabeth Taylor and Richard Burton, Audrey Hepburn, and Princess Grace of Monaco. Birkin represented a new generation of star to be invited, and instead of a typically bohemian ensemble she chose a period-appropriate look by Yves Saint Laurent. The gown, made of pale peach taffeta and chiffon with a high neck, puffed sleeves, and a ruffled hem, was reminiscent of a dress one might have worn a century ago. Gainsbourg also dressed methodically, in a moiré evening coat and trousers. Instead of a bow tie with his white shirt, he wore a short necklace reminiscent of a Maltese cross at the neck and a long chain with a magnifying glass. He wanted to make a splashy arrival in a vintage Rolls-Royce he owned but rarely drove due to the fact he didn't have a license, so they hired a chauffeur. The car was so old it had no heat and no suspension, so Birkin's piled updo kept deflating with every bump in the road. Instead of making their grand entrance, they were directed to a distant parking lot, which made for a long and freezing mid-December walk to the entrance. If she was annoyed at Gainsbourg for prioritizing being seen over ease, she didn't allow herself to remember any lingering resentment. She told a reporter that the night was "a giggle."

In the music they recorded, the older, domineering Gainsbourg was a Svengali type who made most of the artistic decisions with Birkin as his muse. But one area where he did not have final say and in which she was truly confident was in clothes—to the point where it was she, not he, calling the shots, even for his own looks. Birkin was a key architect of Gainsbourg's evolving appearance. He was insecure about how long it took for him to grow a beard but also thought he looked too young without one. Birkin advised a specific amount of stubble: eight days of growth to sculpt his face and create shadows and highlights, like a natural form of makeup. She liked the total lack of hair on his chest and arms and how he adorned himself with diamond tennis bracelets and Cartier bangles and a sapphire pendant necklace—some femininity with all his forceful masculinity. He often wore a Rolex Daytona watch or a Breitling with a custom strap and carried an Hermès Haut à Courroies, a massive bag originally designed to store saddles. This was offset by his aggressively casual daily look, which was largely composed of shirts from the Boy Scouts of America or denim Western-style shirts he would wear unbuttoned to the navel. He wore faded blue jeans, which Birkin instructed would be more erotic if he also skipped underwear entirely. She bought him a white jazz shoe—the style was called Zizi—she found in the sales basket at Repetto, which was a brand of dance-wear and shoes, and they became his signature. She preferred he wear no socks, to show off his delicate ankles.

Birkin molded him into the man of her fantasies, perhaps, because apparel was the only place she was allowed to exert her own aesthetic preferences. It certainly wasn't allowed at home. They had settled into a small house at 5 bis rue de Verneuil in 1970—or, rather, she moved into Gainsbourg's home. He had bought the house in the late 1960s on a little street of seventeenth-century buildings between the boulevard Saint-Germain and the Seine. The tiny house was approximately 1,400 square feet, but its warren of rooms made it feel smaller. "I don't know if it's a studio, a museum, a salon, or a brothel," Gainsbourg said in a French television interview. The neighborhood had a mix of bohemians and academic types. James Baldwin had once lived in dingy hotels on rue de Verneuil, and Jacques Lacan, the famous psychoanalyst, lived a block away. There were plenty of creature comforts for Serge: He had his wine shop, his *tabac* to buy his countless no-filter Gitanes, and his favorite haunts, like Brasserie Lipp and Café de Flore and Bilboquet, all close by.

The understanding between Gainsbourg and Birkin was that she was moving into his home. He had lived there first, and this was his highly personalized domain—the house of a single man. He had covered all the walls in a deep black felt; there was almost no natural light. The floors were black-and-white marble or covered in a black patterned wall-to-wall carpet. He thought it suited his demeanor. "I love melancholy," he said. "I'm not looking for a cure. Daydreaming and melancholy are my drugs."

There was very little privacy. Outside, fans paying homage fresh off the couple's "*Je t'aime*" success were prone to treating the home like a place they were entitled to visit. Gainsbourg had to hire a house manager not just to clean and do the shopping or pick up a pack of cigarettes, but to answer the door to the numerous people who would ring the doorbell. Sometimes they wanted money, or help finding work. If Gainsbourg was in a particularly good mood, he would ask them inside. Press came too. They could be found sorting through the couple's trash outside in case there was anything of note to photograph or write about.

Inside was claustrophobic. "Clutter" was a generous way to put it: hotel ashtrays from the Lancaster and the Raphaël overflowing with cigarette butts; more than one piano; guns and bullets; toy monkeys; Cartier boxes in their signature red; a collection of police badges. Adding to the sense of being trapped in someone's private world, there were lascivious signs of female sexuality everywhere. The walls bore a poster of the film *Lolita* and portraits of collaborators and lovers in Gainsbourg's life, including Anna Karina, Petula Clark, Juliette Gréco, Catherine Deneuve, Isabelle Adjani, Marianne Faithfull, and Françoise Hardy. There were large pictures of both Birkin and Brigitte Bardot. There was even a bronze cast of Birkin's bust. She had to occupy space that was filled with objectification of her and other women, like a version of Bluebeard's castle.

The bedroom looked like that of a bachelor, the kind of place where nothing wholesome had ever happened. The windows: covered in blackout curtains. The walls: black. The bed: gigantic. The coverlet: made of black mink. At the foot of the bed was a bench in the shape of a mermaid.

Nor was the bathroom oriented toward anyone's taste but Gainsbourg's. The bathtub had a low-hanging chandelier above it that would graze an adult or bonk Birkin on the head when she was trying to give Kate a bath. For Gainsbourg, the tub was purely a flourish—he almost never used it. In her diaries Birkin celebrates him finally taking a bath after three months, although she was always quick to assure anyone that he meticulously washed himself via the bidet daily.

The only space for Birkin was a room on the second floor that she considered her boudoir. And it was certainly not a place to raise a child. Gainsbourg didn't want to see a single trace of the au pairs raising Kate Barry anywhere in the living space. And soon there would be a baby to add to the children's room: Birkin was pregnant with her second and Serge's third child.

At first the living arrangement, if quirky, worked for the couple. But there was tension between the rising fame of Birkin in the world and the way her boyfriend viewed her. She could embody his muse creatively, but he was not able to live with her as an equal, someone with her own desires for her home. Gainsbourg simply saw his partner as another one of his possessions.

CHAPTER SEVEN

We Are an Amoral Couple

Jane Birkin found out she was pregnant via a health scare. She had been filming *Romance of a Horsethief*, an adventure film set at the turn of the century starring Yul Brynner, in which she played the titular Robin Hood–style folk hero's love interest, Naomi. The role was a career highlight—she had grown up watching *The Ten Commandments*, in which Brynner had starred, with her family. Serge Gainsbourg had a smaller role in the film as a rebel villager, and they had been ensconced along with little Kate in Zagreb, filming for much of the second half of 1970. While there, Gainsbourg developed a new and exhausting party trick. At a little pub in a tiny village, drunk on vodka, he would rail against the country's communist regime and set fire to the local currency. Birkin was less focused on his behavior than her own insecurity, which came out as blazing jealousy of the busty, dark-haired Italian and Yugoslavian women who were working on *Romance of a Horsethief*, paranoid that Gainsbourg would be lured into cheating.

After shooting, they decided to drive to Venice, where they had spent time when they were shooting *Slogan* in the heady early days of their romance. Birkin had severe abdominal pain the entire ride and suspected it might be a cyst. She ignored the pain in favor of spending three days in a hotel bedroom with Gainsbourg while Kate indulged in chasing pigeons, one of her favorite activities, with her nanny.

Back in Paris a few days later, Birkin went to her gynecologist, who thought she might have appendicitis but also made her take a pregnancy test just in case. She got a call later that day that not only was she pregnant, but the doctor thought she might be having an ectopic pregnancy. Despite the severity of the situation, Birkin wanted a second opinion, and wanted it to come from a doctor in London. She arrived the next night at the London Clinic, where both she and Kate had been born, and was diagnosed with a healthy pregnancy but acute appendicitis. It was all a shock, but she was fine, and on January 21, 1971, after she was stabilized, she wrote in her journal about how being surrounded by her parents, her brother Andrew, her sister Linda, and, most of all, Gainsbourg had filled her with comfort. Contentedness did not always last long in their emotionally volatile relationship.

She felt deeply protective of his fragility. Just a few months after the appendicitis incident, in April 1971, Gainsbourg got a call from his sister Jacqueline that his father was dying. He had seemed fine until he complained of indigestion and began to cough up blood. The family sent for a doctor and for Gainsbourg. By the time he arrived, his father had already died. Birkin had never seen a face show so much pain and felt out of her depth, both because she had never experienced the death of someone so close to her and because she was pregnant and had been told to stay at home, but she wanted to go to the hospital and see the Gainsbourg family as they grieved.

Despite all the tumult, Birkin and Gainsbourg continued their creative collaboration. It grew along with the love affair, to the point where their romance and their artistry were indistinguishable. Their 1971 album *Histoire de Melody Nelson* was Gainsbourg and Birkin at their charismatic peak. It was a concept album whose running time was less than half an hour, centered on Melody Nelson, a Lolita-esque fourteen-year-old girl who gets romanced by the album's narrator—a middle-aged man who seems quite close in character to Gainsbourg—and then dies in a plane crash. The concept crafted around the record was barely passable according to the sexual mores of the time, but that didn't stop the album from being critically regarded as Gainsbourg's masterwork.

Birkin appears on just one track: "Ballade de Melody Nelson," but her essence is all over the album. It was Gainsbourg's first true rock 'n' roll album, no longer candy pop or cabaret-influenced *chanson française.* It was his equivalent of Bob Dylan going electric. That interest in rock came from Birkin. Gainsbourg had come of age in the late 1940s and '50s. He was a piano man at heart. She, on the other hand, was a child of '60s London who had come of age with the ascendance of rock music.

Birkin seemed unbothered by the album's risqué themes, which were now old hat for Gainsbourg. She tended to laugh off his attempts to rile up his audience. She even posed for the cover image in a red wig and unbuttoned jeans, holding her monkey toy, which she used to hide her stomach. (She is early enough along in the photo that she looks pregnant only if you already know.) The real-life twenty-four-year-old Birkin posing as a fourteen-year-old while pregnant was the kind of inside joke that Gainsbourg delighted in. He showed over and over that he was uninterested in morality. He was, however, interested in shocking people.

And Birkin herself enjoyed shocking those around her. Just because she was pregnant did not mean she had any intention of toning down her brand of provocation. During her third trimester, when she was visibly pregnant, she went for a walk wearing a dress that barely skimmed the tops of her thighs with bright green—almost fluorescent—underpants. A man on boulevard Saint-Germain stopped her and asked whether she was ashamed of herself. "*Pas du tout*," she said. Not at all.

At seven months pregnant, in May 1971, she and Gainsbourg went to Japan to do press for *Cannabis* (or *The Mafia Wants Blood*, the title in English), a B-level crime movie the two had filmed in 1970. It was not well received; Gainsbourg played a hit man working for the Mafia, and Birkin acted as the rich daughter of an ambassador who spends much of the film naked. However, despite the chilly reception to the film itself, Birkin was greeted by mobs of people everywhere she went, playing "Je t'aime . . . moi non plus." At a Tokyo press conference, the room was lined with hundreds of people, including thirty photographers, and a mass of reporters and interpreters crowded around a half dozen microphones. She was unconcerned with the risks and, in her diaries, truly laid-back about traveling around the globe during a late pregnancy. She mentioned how flattered she was by the attention, complimenting how well organized the trip was and how delicious she found Japanese food.

In June 1971, just a few weeks after they had arrived back in Paris from Japan, Birkin's sister Linda called and said, in a shaky voice, that their father had a tumor that might be cancerous. His doctor had said not to worry and they would operate in a few days, but Birkin and Gainsbourg left immediately to fly to London. It was a tender time for the couple: Gainsbourg's own father had died just six weeks prior. From his hospital bed, the elder Birkin said he wished she would have the baby then, several weeks early, so he could meet the child in case he didn't survive. He also told his daughter that he'd been so physically ill when she married John Barry at eighteen that it led to an ulcer. Birkin blamed the pills he was taking for his cruel statement, but that didn't stop the guilt from gnawing at her. "The one person in the world I would've moved heaven and earth never to hurt," she wrote, adding that he requested one thing: a photograph of his beloved Serge Gainsbourg by his bed. Gainsbourg was reluctant to leave but had to return to Paris for a week to work and to check on the emotional state of his mother, who he thought needed as much distraction as possible after her husband's death. Birkin's father's health was improving, but he was still in a London hospital convalescing, and so she wanted to give birth in London as she had with Kate.

When she went into labor in London in July 1971, she was shy enough to keep Gainsbourg out of the birthing room. "If he had seen me giving birth," she wrote, "it's possible he never would have slept with me again, and I wasn't taking that chance." Instead, that night Birkin's brother and Gainsbourg drank through all the liquor at the hotel bar, down to the banana liqueur. She named her daughter Charlotte Lucy Gainsbourg after her old friend the actress Charlotte Rampling.

Charlotte was born with jaundice and was taken to Middlesex Hospital for a transfusion, where she was registered as Baby Birkin. Birkin told the staff to watch for an odd-looking man with a five-o'clock shadow, hair askew, and an anxious look in his eyes who quite possibly smelled of banana liqueur. She was joking, a little, and compensating for Gainsbourg's heavy drinking. Nonetheless when Gainsbourg showed up to the postnatal intensive care, he had trouble being admitted to the unit because staff thought he looked suspicious.

When Birkin had given birth to Kate Barry in 1967, she was just a little bit famous, part of the London scene but not someone whose pregnancy or birth would be covered by the media. In just four years, her circumstances had changed. News of her pregnancy with Charlotte had been covered in pop culture magazines like *Paris Jour* and *Bonne Soirée* in 1971 with headlines like "Maternité = Mariage" ("Motherhood = Marriage"). Birkin was easygoing as always, and so wrapped up in her own excitement about her two daughters and Gainsbourg that she did not take time to reflect on how this round of motherhood might be different for her.

She was, however, quite self-aware about being a living embodiment of a laissez-faire style of parenting. They took the girls wherever they went: bringing the kids along to a party, letting them eat late and go to sleep while their parents were still carousing, even if it seemed like a place a baby would be bored or, worse, not welcome. At restaurants, the couple felt the derision of fellow diners judging the famous, scandalous couple with an angelic blond toddler and a baby in tow. Birkin was proud of their lack of taboos. "We weren't the Kennedys! . . . The twenty-year age gap, our lifestyle," she said. "Serge used to say: 'We are not an immoral couple, we are an amoral couple.'" Some of their unconventional parenting was the result of a blithe disregard for what they considered middle-class values. At the same time, they were coasting along on the elevated status of being rich and famous, feeling like traditional social norms didn't apply to them.

The carefree-looking family was photographed by a Côte d'Azur paparazzo, James Andanson, in 1972 on holiday in the South of France: Gainsbourg holding the hand of Kate, who is wearing a forced smile and a pinafore, toddling alongside her mother, carrying Charlotte. Wholesome, until you see the parents' aesthetic choices:

Birkin in short denim cutoffs and Gainsbourg in a pair of jeans and an unbuttoned denim jacket, bare chest out.

Andrew Birkin continued being the family's resident photographer; there's a shot he took in 1970 of Kate one evening at a restaurant called Les Vapeurs in Trouville in Normandy in which the toddler looks like she's having an existential crisis. "Kate has a look in turns interrogative, bored, sad, curious, and happy—entirely Kate," wrote Andrew. That same year, Birkin brought Kate to a casino dressed in a black velvet dress with a white organza ruffled collar. She claimed Kate was taken with a violinist, swaying to the Russian music. They would occasionally bring baby Charlotte to a nightclub, toting her around in one of Birkin's famous basket bags.

Birkin was raised in a nuclear family unit that was close on an emotional level but one that was more typical of the English upper crust, being looked after by nannies while her parents were in the land of adults and then being sent away to school at a young age. Birkin and Gainsbourg's compromise, if it can even be called one, was to choose to be hands-on with the kids *and* have an active social life. They wanted to be a steady presence.

Birkin and Gainsbourg saw parenting as an act of collaboration, just as their creative lives were. On nights when they didn't want to bring the girls along or they had school the next morning, the couple had a routine. After the girls went to bed, they would go to the usual haunts like Régine's or Raspoutine or Élysée-Matignon or Le Castel, where they would drink, chain-smoke, and dance until the wee hours, the night often ending with Gainsbourg playing songs on the piano for the crowd. Kate called their coterie "the court of nighttime jerks." Around dawn, Birkin and Gainsbourg would come home to the house on rue de Verneuil to get the girls up at 7 a.m. and off to school, then sleep until about two in the afternoon, drink coffee—sometimes spiked with cognac—and pick them up from school. Undoubtedly, Birkin stood out from the other mothers. When Charlotte Gainsbourg was seven or eight, she remembered, Birkin came to pick her up from school while wearing a skintight blue sequined dress. "She was so glamorous, so beautiful," Charlotte said. This was not a totally unusual arrangement for their social circle—

they raised the girls in an enclave of fellow wealthy, jet-set people who traveled frequently and who liked a night out and adult time. Still, this did not shield the couple from scorn from even their daughters. Classmates of Kate and Charlotte would ring the bell of their house just to see if Birkin would answer the door naked. Birkin knew it was difficult for her girls but never seemed inclined to conform to a more conservative version of family life—not for them, and certainly not for other parents: "I think for Kate and Charlotte, it was not very funny to have parents so shocking. For the other parents who said bad things about us . . . Over time, it all faded away."

Famous women—and, really, all women—are faced with the choice of whether to retreat from public life at a certain point in their careers if they wish to have children. Or rather, it's not a choice at all—having a child, no matter how many resources one has, requires a series of compromises. Birkin chose her career and fame again and again but refused to do so at the cost of her children. She was making the same calculations all women do in order to determine if they can manage to have it all. In that sense she was a trailblazer, refusing to slow down or adhere to typical conventions of motherhood. She was a woman with an incredible ability to take life in stride and keep blithely moving forward. But she would eventually have to slow down to grapple with her own emotional state.

CHAPTER EIGHT

I Chucked Myself into the Seine

In 1974, Jane Birkin and Serge Gainsbourg appeared together in a cheeky ad campaign for Léo Isba belts. The ads ran in fashion magazines as a double-page spread on facing pages. There's a photo of a naked torso with a big black belt wrapped around it, its owner tying another belt around a wrist in a pose suggestive of domination. On the left page it reads, "Belts are like women: the best accessories," and is signed by Serge Gainsbourg. And on the right, it reads "*Salaud!*" meaning "swine" or, less literally, "bastard," and is signed by Jane Birkin. The ad was another iteration of the couple's fondness for pushing boundaries. It also encapsulated their individual personas. Gainsbourg was prone to making broadly misogynistic statements to the press. This was a man who said on a Swiss radio show in 1968, the year he met Birkin, that miniskirts were a scourge on society, as opposed to 1930 when women had "modesty in public." It certainly didn't apply to his girlfriend's style. Birkin acted like his presentation was all an exaggeration of his personality and that she was game to play his foil no matter what. She served to lighten the mood but was not shy about pushing back at him. In the context of a fashion magazine, the ad comes off as impudent, maybe even a little voyeuristic, like the person flipping pages was witnessing foreplay.

The antagonism in their relationship could take the form of a public spectacle. A widely told story about an argument they had around 1970 demonstrates this dynamic. They were drinking—"plastered," Birkin said—at Castel's and were walking home along the

Seine, arguing about some long-lost point. Tensions escalated, and she dove into the river to avoid his berating. Plus it gave the fight a big, cathartic finish. Gainsbourg paused to take his watch off before getting her out, and the river police got to her first. When Birkin retold the incident in interviews, she played it for laughs, always noting that they walked home arm in arm, and the worst result was that the Yves Saint Laurent blouse she was wearing shrank when it dried.

The truth is that their fights would on occasion turn violent. In one such incident in the early '70s Birkin and Gainsbourg were in a nightclub in Paris. She details it in her diary:

"I think he was mentioning the name of some girl, actress or something. I slapped him, lightly and funnily, I thought, and he hit out at my left eye like mad so I hid my head for at least half an hour, my eyes running like a river," she wrote. The argument quickly escalated into a public scene. She reached for her basket bag and he turned it upside down, spilling out the contents onto the floor of the club. "Then I made a grab for my basket and Serge turned it over; everything out, all over the floor at Castel's. Needless to say mad embarrassment. Then [I began] to pick everything up, furious, and jabbed at him with my cigarette still slightly alight. So he bashed me again and tore me down by my hair and slapped me again and left the nightclub." She was stunned and upset but she also blamed herself, finding her behavior ugly and the whole thing embarrassing. She stayed at Castel's for half an hour drinking whisky while listening to gawkers gossiping about her in French; joking that a tabloid reporter should have caught it, thinking she couldn't understand what they were saying.

In her rush to leave this situation, Birkin forgot her cape and book back at the club. When she arrived home after trying to flag down a few taxis who wouldn't take her in her state, she was crying. Gainsbourg dragged her upstairs, where she threw up all over the bed. She seemed proud to report in her diary that Gainsbourg cared for her: "Serge was so kind and gentle. I felt so sick about myself," she wrote. "He was an angel but a human too." They spent the next day, Sunday, alone in bed together.

Some of her own accounts of these famous quarrels vary wildly. In this one, sometimes she left out the other woman's name and the slapping and just said that they were drunk at Castel's and that the overturned bag was part of some other disagreement. "I was so ashamed and horrified that everyone could see everything! In a rather drunk mood, I put it all back in, itching for revenge," she said in one interview. "In less than no time, I got my hands on a lemon custard pie that I chucked at Serge." Sometimes this story is merged with the dive into the Seine. "I thought I had done something so shameful that I really had to do something pretty extraordinary: I raced past him and went straight down the Rue des Saints-Pères to the river and then I chucked myself into the Seine! I had to be fished out by firemen, it had quite a strong current!" she said. "Serge was in a forgiving mood like anything—I mean really. All was forgiven."

Her reading of Gainsbourg's essential nature also seemed to change in different depictions, perhaps in trying to write her own sunny and optimistic narrative about her partner: Sometimes he could be childlike, other times clownish. They were the most famous couple—most famous family, really—in France. Her love for him was all-consuming in a way that is usually associated with adolescence or first love. Even as she grew more recognizable for her acting and creative contributions, her private ruminations were more concerned with her emotional state around her relationship than with her career. As much as she was a celebrity with great social currency, Birkin was not very independent. She had never lived alone; she was not able to cultivate much sense of self outside of her relationships with men and her children. She went out often, so she had plenty of people she was friendly with, but she was limited in whom she had deep involvement with. She relied on her parents, siblings, daughters, and, most of all, Gainsbourg, despite the volatility.

In 1973, at age forty-five, Serge Gainsbourg had a heart attack. Birkin was filming a movie in Paris called *Projection privée* (*Private Screening*), about a director making a movie about his wife's suicide. When she heard the news, she rushed to his side at the American Hospital. Gainsbourg didn't take the health scare very seriously.

When Birkin arrived at his room, she found he had unplugged his heart monitor and was making "ghastly" sounds. He joked to Birkin that he certainly might live longer if he gave up smoking, but life might seem so long then, and so boring.

News of the heart attack plastered the news; Gainsbourg even made the cover of *France-Soir* for his emergency. Birkin was ready to raise hell about the tabloids having no respect for what he was going through until he blushed and admitted he had called them himself.

The heart attack scared him, even if he made light of it to Jane. In its aftermath he wrote one of his saddest and most personal songs, "Je suis venu te dire que je m'en vais" ("I Came to Tell You I'm Leaving"), in which he tells Birkin and Charlotte "Farewell forever."

For Birkin, the heart attack was a reminder of how fleeting life could be. She wrote, "I was so worried when Serge was in that blasted hospital and I thought people were lying and he would be dead. I remember screaming and worrying how many sleeping pills I had got. If Serge is dead, I want to die too."

The crisis had come as *Di doo dah*, her debut solo album, was released. Her voice was still considered weak or, at least, an acquired taste, like her strong English accent in speaking French; it was always hard to tell if she was playing it up or this was natural. She could be seen as untalented or wholly unique or both. And Gainsbourg, who had written or cowritten each of the songs, got most of the artistic credit along with Jean-Claude Vannier, the producer who added string arrangements and organs to the sensual wash of the songs. The title track was about her flat chest, and "Help camionneur" was a horny song about a truck driver.

The closest thing they had to a party for the album was at a country hotel in Brittany, which had invited everyone—it was printed in the local paper—for a lamb roast with a note that Gainsbourg and Birkin would be attending. The locals wanted them to sing "Di doo dah," and when the famous couple said they didn't want to, the hotel just blared it on loudspeakers. It's not that Birkin wasn't excited about the album; she toured for it and did press, and the songs stayed in her singing repertoire for the rest of her life. But in appearances like the one on the British *Russell Harty Show* in September 1973, she joked about how her breasts were so flat she was sometimes jealous of men, and then sing-whispered her single "Di doo dah" in her now signature way. She came across as a giggly eternal girl, which didn't really do anything to push the public's perception of her as a serious artist.

Her ardor for Gainsbourg was as strong as ever, but she also began to privately ruminate on commitment. In the mid-'70s, about six years into their liaison, their relationship began to fracture and jealousy further crept in. Many women, according to her, but particularly "bosomy" starlets, were throwing themselves at Gainsbourg. She wondered to herself if he'd had affairs but thought he was too smart to let on about them in any way. If he cheated, she maintained in her diaries, her feelings would not change; she would love him, she would be hurt, but she would not leave him.

Despite this declaration, she was also grappling with curiosity about what it would be like to be with someone else. In November 1974, a man she would identify only as "C." wanted to be her "friend." "Everyone has been unfaithful but I haven't. So why should I suffer for what I haven't done? . . . I don't want to spoil my thing with Serge," she wrote in November 1974 about her partner's flip cruelty. She was jealous that he didn't hesitate to check out seventeen-year-old girls in front of her. And she, at twenty-seven, with two kids, was feeling like perhaps she was aging out of his interest. He even took to calling her *ma vieille*, my old lady. She felt like she was constantly one mistake away from being traded in for a new, younger model of woman. She would be devastated and he would just start again.

The two never did get married, though they did consider having a big wedding at the Gare de Lyon train station at one point. The press was fascinated by the will-they-or-won't-they dynamic. Andrew Birkin took a black-and-white photo of Gainsbourg in 1974 reading a newspaper headline about himself in which he said about Birkin, "You are not my wife, darling—I love my liberty too much." Freedom was never something Birkin seemed interested in taking from Gainsbourg.

Birkin was mildly enthusiastic about the prospect of marriage, even if she didn't raise it with Gainsbourg. "Of course, I often want to get married. I mean the sort of moments when you think it might be nice to sort of rush off and do it," she wrote. But then she allowed herself to think of the married couples she knew; even the ones who hadn't gotten divorced and were doing fine still said how much of an adjustment it was. "They say, 'Yes the first year it's great fun and everything, and then after that, well it grows into something else.' I don't want it to grow into something else. I want it like it is now and I don't want it to change. I don't want one person to have sort of to get less faithful to you, even just a tiny bit. I don't want anything less than what it is now."

Gainsbourg recovered enough from the heart attack to start working on a script in 1974 for a feature film also called *Je t'aime moi non plus*. He went on to direct the film, which was released in 1976. "Its premise is a tad out of left field, even for him," wrote a *New York Times* critic when it was restored in 2019. The film starred Joe Dallesandro, who had been part of Andy Warhol's scene in New York, as a gay garbage hauler named Krassky (a.k.a. Krass) who is on the road in the wild west of the United States with his immature and loutish lover, Padovan. Birkin, who didn't have any role in the creative development, played a truck stop waitress named Johnny whose boyish looks delighted Krass. (Gainsbourg specified that she cut her hair very short and wear men's undershirts for the movie so she would appear different than in her other films.) In *Je t'aime moi non plus*, her character was a mute sort of sexual slave. A love affair with tragic complications unfolds. Wrote the *New York Times*, "Save for some silly whip-panning in a sequence leading up to an auto accident, he doesn't put a foot wrong. His style is languorous, though, and while the movie is peppered with raw humor, he's serious to a fault in depicting his couple's predicament.

The picture . . . is not for everybody. But it's genuinely, eccentrically Gainsbourgian."

The film was neither a box office nor a critical hit, but it did have a crucial champion in the formidable French New Wave director François Truffaut, he of *The 400 Blows*, *Day for Night*, and *Jules and Jim* fame. When it was released, it played at one of the grand cinemas on the Champs-Élysées, while Birkin complained that in other countries, like her native England, they played it in red-light districts. (It went on to become a cult classic of queer cinema.) What it did cement for her was that she had made the correct artistic choice to stay in France.

For promotion, stills from the movie that simulated penetration were published in Italian *Playboy*. It was not the first time she'd appeared in racy centerfolds. Birkin chose to pose for pornographic magazines like *Lui* ("for the modern man"), where she was shot chained to a bed for the December 1974 Christmas issue. "It's a vision imbued with too much humour to be 'libertine' and too refined to be simply 'dirty,'" she said of the *Lui* artistic direction. The year prior, in *Lui*'s festive issue in 1973, Birkin posed with none other than Brigitte Bardot to promote their film *Don Juan 73*, directed by Bardot's ex Roger Vadim. "I was much more intrigued by Bardot. I wanted to see every portion of her body to see if she was as beautiful as I thought she was, and she is. Checked from head to toe by me," Birkin said. "There's not one fault in the woman."

Her frequent appearances nude in photos and in films was a way to play out the sexual politics of the day—to see how far the touted sexual liberation of the period really went. She appeared in more talked-about shoots, including one spread in *Lui* where Gainsbourg simulates hitting her. Birkin saw these sessions as empowering. "I can't speak for my era," she said later. "The other girls were much freer than I was. There was no one more impressed by a man than I was. I was delighted to be Serge's object of desire, the person who inspired him. I was happy to take naked pictures. To be in *Playboy*, even though I wasn't their type at all. I was a kind of object and that's what I wanted to be." Birkin was in control of her own objectification, in other words, and she wanted the world to know it.

Birkin was ahead of her time in living the kind of liberated life that allowed her to publicly enjoy sex on her own terms. After a childhood of being bullied for her body, being a sex object was something she said she desired for herself. "You said you're the first sex symbol with 'big teeth, bad legs, and no bust.' . . . You reckon that's a fair account?" an interviewer once asked her. Birkin replied with self-effacing humor: "Yes, I'm just touting them up. Somebody took the measurements once and then they thought they must have got me wrong and turned me upside down because they thought this bit should be here [points to her hips, then to her chest], because all the numbers sounded better."

Her thoughts on nudity seemed to vary over the years. In her diary she wrote, "I hate complete nudity, I think it's a bore. I don't find it one jot sexy. I do photos that are sexy, not nude." In interviews she repeated that she thought posing naked or nearly naked was normal and something most actresses did. In another interview, she said, "I find it hilarious, posing nude in *Lui*. I never found it bad. Plus I was very moral. I didn't ask for payment or to intervene in the choice of photos that were published. I don't find naked girls indecent, nor the gentlemen." She compared it to going to the Rodin Museum and enjoying looking at the sculptures' buttocks. She appeared nude cradling daughters Kate and Charlotte on the cover of the Brazilian magazine *Manchete* in September 1974. Her nudity was meant to convey earth mother rather than eroticism, whether or not it was successful.

She was not always so magnanimous about sex, nudity, and intimacy. In 1979, when Birkin was thirty-two, she wrote an open letter about sex and love in her diary to her daughter Kate, who was going through puberty. It was framed as a birds-and-bees talk. One topic she was touched on was pornography. She warned her that magazines could be a source of false impressions about female sexuality—especially ones written by men. "'I touched her nipple and she came like a volcano.' Well, my angel, good luck to all who sail in her, but it's not always true!" In that same letter Birkin suggested that Kate only date men worthy of her love and her brain.

Gone in that moment was the woman who posed for *Lui* magazine whom the world viewed chained to a bed. In her place was Birkin naked in a totally different way, as an earnest but shy mother giving a shot at The Talk. As Birkin aged into her adulthood, the gulf between how the public regarded her and how she felt as a woman only increased.

CHAPTER NINE

Ex Fan des Sixties

Jane Birkin appeared on a Swiss talk show in 1976. The set was stark, just an undecorated studio and a table with a pack of cigarettes and an ashtray on it. Birkin was facing the camera, smoking and wearing a white T-shirt with a stretched-out collar and blue jeans. The man interviewing her, Christian Defaye, asked her in French if she took cinema seriously. "Yes," she said. Then he asked if cinema took *her* seriously. "No," she replied immediately, and grimaced.

Birkin was notorious for her romances and ubiquitous in tabloids and fashion magazines. After *Di doo dah*, she continued to put out solo albums—still written by Gainsbourg—such as 1978's *Ex fan des sixties*, which was well received in France but far from the breakout hits "Je t'aime . . . moi non plus" and "Ballade de Melody Nelson" the decade prior. Her acting work was not where she wanted it to be. Since *Blow-Up*, she had been typecast as sexy-yet-ditzy girls or romantic interests who had little to do on-camera other than look the part. Her work was largely in Europe and mostly in French-language films, many immediately obscure, including *La moutarde me monte au nez*, *La course à l'échalote*, *The Devil in the Heart*, and *19 Girls and a Sailor*. Birkin joked that if someone was a fan of Benny Hill, they might find them funny, suggesting the films were not the most sophisticated or challenging. Her image was cemented as a talent, but not the kind that was ever nominated for acting awards. There was plenty of work, but she remained somewhat unknown as an actress outside France or continental Europe.

When she finally was cast in a role in a big English-language film, it was still as an ingénue even though she was thirty. She played a maid in the all-star adaptation of Agatha Christie's whodunit *Death on the Nile* in 1978. She enjoyed being on set and was a keen observer of her fellow actors and crew. The *Death on the Nile* cast included Maggie Smith and Mia Farrow; they all stayed together at the Oberoi Hotel in Egypt. For Birkin it was a big break. She was crestfallen to hear that not all of the cast felt that way. At dinner Maggie Smith announced, "I'm only doing this for cash. I haven't even read the script." The cash must have been good enough because she was subsequently cast, as was Birkin as a lavishly dressed wife, in another Christie adaptation, *Evil Under the Sun*, in 1982. Those roles proved that Birkin was not intimidated by acting alongside legends in her field. And even amid the slightly camp tone of the film, she held her own, whispering "I can't bear to be pitied" to Peter Ustinov's detective Poirot in *Evil Under the Sun* and making it seem believable.

Her acting career was certainly prolific, but the roles she landed often lacked substance or an opportunity for Birkin to showcase her talents. She had become increasingly insecure about her work, constantly comparing herself in her journals to other actresses like Nastassja Kinski and Fanny Ardant, both of whom she regarded as being more beautiful, more talented, and more courageous in their craft. She worked steadily, but she was living through the 1970s boom time for auteurist directors. Around the time she turned thirty, she wanted to be cast against type and challenged. Diane Keaton had a somewhat analogous kooky public persona to Birkin's, but she still managed to get cast in instant classics like *The Godfather* and *Annie Hall*. Birkin's professional aspirations were also an indication that she was beginning to explore her life beyond being half of a relationship.

In the summer of 1979, a friend suggested she try out for a role in the movie *La fille prodigue* (*The Prodigal Daughter*), by the director Jacques Doillon. Birkin chose to meet him at her home on the rue de Verneuil in her room, the one part of the house that had her own belongings and her personality. He was thirty-five to her thirty-two years old and had been directing his own movies since the early 1970s. He had a quiet, intellectual bearing compared to Gainsbourg's man-of-the-streets energy. He was funny and an attentive listener, and, like Birkin, cared deeply about the technical aspects of filmmaking. Doillon's style was known as naturalistic; the role she was auditioning for was a woman in her thirties going through a deep depression.

Everything about it was tantalizing, including Doillon himself, to whom she felt an immediate attraction. But she also had her misgivings. She was not a cheater. Disentangling herself from Gainsbourg would take a long time. And what she wanted was to be taken seriously, not to get the role because of an affair or to jump into another relationship with a creator and his muse dynamic. That summer of 1979 she wrote, "Maybe I even kissed Jacques, to his surprise, I so wanted him to find me interesting just for me." The "maybe" is doing a lot of work here—almost like an erotic fantasy. Did she resist? Did he? She could not even bring herself to write out the details.

They did start up a clandestine affair that summer of 1979. When she was in London seeing her family, Doillon flew to Heathrow Airport. Birkin had Gabrielle Crawford, her dearest friend—who she knew would never tell Gainsbourg or the press—drive her out to Heathrow so they could meet up for a two-hour visit before he flew home to Paris.

During the affair, Birkin was becoming conscious of her own autonomy, and starting to assert her own desires. The fantasy she allowed herself to engage in, of some happy *ménage à trois* where she had her longtime partner and a lover on the side, was not one she was going to realistically achieve, but she played it out as long as she could. For six months of their torrid affair, she would push into even more daring territory, sending Doillon telegrams asking him to marry her. He responded that he wanted to marry her too.

She also got the role in *The Prodigal Daughter*. If she had to reconcile that with the desire to be seen seriously, she never showed it. Instead, she felt she had triumphed on two counts: a new lover and a meaty role that could show her range as an actress. The affair proceeded through filming in June 1980 in Calvados, in Normandy. When they were finished, Doillon gave her a parting ultimatum: that he wanted her to be happy if she went back to Gainsbourg—but she had better be truly happy, not go back to her old life of being drunk at four in the morning in a nightclub surrounded by famous people. The Birkin he'd thought he was meeting was the lounge lizard whose role of Gainsbourg muse had been established. The woman he was having an affair with had turned out to be more thoughtful and ambitious. Doillon was saying that he thought she had evolved beyond that old life.

But Birkin was not ready to simply renounce the nightlife. The parties made her feel independent and alive. In May 1980, Birkin and Gainsbourg had gone out for the actor Armel Issartel's birthday. That evening there were so many celebrities present that even Birkin felt like she couldn't stop gawking. Mikhail Baryshnikov was drinking like a fish; Roman Polanski was jolly and impish; Christina Onassis was in one corner, Mick Jagger in another. Jagger teased Birkin about her heavy British accent (which was either flirtatious or showed a staggering amount of delusion, considering Jagger's own French is heavily accented and a little halting). In a break from the normal routine, Gainsbourg went home early. Birkin stayed out without him, which was unusual for her. It was a small rebellion for her to go out dancing with Baryshnikov at La Calavados and Paradis Latin, driving the wrong way on one-way streets around the Left Bank until she got home at 7 a.m.

Birkin was torn. She loved Gainsbourg but was tired of their shared drama and his alcoholism. Since the days when he brought a gun while she was filming *La piscine*, he'd been fond of threatening to kill anyone who got in between them. Maybe once it had seemed chivalrous, but, over a decade into their relationship, it was just another example of Gainsbourg's darkness. He said to her just two days prior that she was the love of his life, something he had never told anyone before. In late May 1980, she wrote in her diary that his ardor was possessive, telling her, "You're mine and I will kill anyone who tries to take you away. I will excuse all your mistakes, for better or for worse. I am your unconditional love. I am an unconditional of Jane." She was wary of his histrionics but she still did love him.

Relations between Birkin and Gainsbourg continued to devolve, careening toward some kind of split. She returned from filming to Serge and his house in Paris, which she still didn't legally own any part of despite living there for a decade. More and more frequently he went out alone. She didn't know if he was also cheating or if he was too much of a drunk to be that calculating. She often slept alone in his massive fur blanket–covered bed, and when he came home at dawn he would pass out not on the sofa downstairs or in his office but in her room. If she tried to talk to him the next day about coming home late, he would tell her she was a bore.

While still pining for Doillon, Birkin could muster despair over Gainsbourg. "I wish for a pill, so I don't have to go on," she wrote. Another day she told herself, "I sometimes want to die very much and by his hand." She failed to resist the urge to defend him, despite her pain. "I must stress that I was absolutely not a battered woman. . . . In fact, he was not at all a violent man," she wrote in her diaries. And yet there was violence in the relationship—not just Gainsbourg's bad temper, but real physical violence. That, and her tendency toward melancholy and suicidal ideation, cannot be denied. In a rare moment of accountability, Serge Gainsbourg once called his behavior abusive, even if she would not use any synonym of that word. "I was too abusive. I came home completely pissed, I beat her. When she gave me an earful, I didn't like it: two seconds too much and bam! . . . she took it on the chin with me."

At the age of thirty-three, what Birkin wanted was to finally have a little peace, agency, and time to herself. She wanted, she confided in her journals, a house full of sunlight, a garden for her girls to play in. She didn't want to take orders from a man old enough to be her father or be told what was acceptable and what was forbidden. She wanted a life without fear or shame. She knew that dream wasn't attainable while she stayed with Gainsbourg. She was less afraid of him and more resigned to the kind of person he was: someone who would always have an almost pathological desire to be in control. Nothing about leaving Gainsbourg would be neat or easy.

But she was bored and worried she wasn't living up to her own aspirations. Even her young daughters could tell she was depressed, and that pushed Birkin toward action. Birkin wrote in her diary that needing to care for children scared her. "When you have a child, you have a purpose, and when things go wrong, you have to do something for this little person who says: 'Mom, get up, why are you sad, what are we eating for lunch?' You have to find them something to eat."

Gainsbourg considered her his creation. She had been a willing participant in this dynamic for years, but now she wanted to break free. She'd once laughed off her partner's antics; now she no longer felt amused by him at all. She felt disgust for Gainsbourg's sense of superiority, for how proud of himself he always was, how sure he was of his own talent and glory, how easily flattered he was by sycophants. He acted like writing a song for someone was the same as doling out a winning lottery ticket. She could no longer tolerate his aggression and violence and how he normalized extreme behavior. After twelve years together, she was at a breaking point.

Birkin was not scared of what would happen if they stayed together; what she really feared was how she would be seen in the world as just Jane. She had built a life for herself in Paris, but it was still Gainsbourg's world. She had no idea what her Paris might look like without him. In late July 1980, she and Doillon fought in plain sight at the Élysées-Matignon hotel, which was a place her social set frequented. Everyone—*le tout Paris*—could see that something was going on between them; so-called friends went so far as to telephone Gainsbourg and ask him, "Do you know about Jacques and Jane?" She felt ashamed for cheating, but she felt more ashamed that she wasn't making up her mind to break up with Serge or to stay.

In the fall of 1980, Jane Birkin finally decided to leave Serge Gainsbourg. From her interpretation, their separation was not tied to one big fight or one affair, but an accumulation of arguments they'd had over and over. Their dynamic was never going to change. Gainsbourg didn't wish for it to; that was the problem.

The timing finally felt right—he was busy recording an album with Catherine Deneuve. When Birkin told Gainsbourg her plan to leave, there was no violent fight. Their breakup was dignified; it had an elegiac quality. When the press got wind of the news, they treated it like a scandal. "The Mysterious 'Divorce' of Serge Gainsbourg and Jane Birkin" was the headline in *France Dimanche* in October 1980. That same month *Paris Match* ran a photo of Birkin in a white dress with her daughters with the article "Serge and Jane: The End of a Love of 12 Years."

Birkin no longer wanted to be told what to do, and she didn't want to just be a beautiful girl to Gainsbourg and to the public. When they met, she was a twenty-year-old who knew nothing about the world, in his eyes—someone who could be molded to perfection. Either he knew she wasn't that girl anymore and could no longer assert his dominance over her as she realized this, or he was incapable of seeing her as anyone other than the girl with the bad French who was auditioning for *Slogan*. But the truth was, Birkin had grown up—and she was ready to show the world who she really was.

CHAPTER TEN
The New Jane

The filming of *The Prodigal Daughter*, over the summer of 1980, was arduous. Jane Birkin was cast as Anne, a woman in her thirties in such a deep depression that she leaves her husband and goes to live with her parents. Discovering that her father (played by the French actor Michel Piccoli) is having an affair, Anne feels jealous of his mistress and grows possessive of and attached to him. It's a psychological drama with some deeply Freudian-influenced themes of love and maybe slightly incestuous feelings for one's parents. It's an upsetting premise, but the film is more subtle than salacious, contemplating how much children have to suffer for the actions of their parents. The film, directed by Birkin's new love, Jacques Doillon, would succeed or fail squarely on Birkin's performance.

"I hate this film," she wrote in her diary in July 1980, worrying that every decision she made in her scenes was wrong, missing her daughters while she was on set in Normandy, even wondering if God existed. Birkin never spoke about the research she did for roles or what her artistic process was to get into character, but she had hit an emotional limit. This role is mostly quiet, both in tone and in its long pauses and stretches with little or no dialogue. Birkin signals her character's pain in the way she reluctantly eats spoonfuls of food and the somnambulant way she shuffles around, as if she's always waking up from amnesia. "No one had ever offered me a part like that or asked me to have a nervous breakdown. . . . I completely let go. I was suddenly allowed to go ballistic on screen," she said.

Doillon didn't want polished performances—he wanted accidents, anything raw from doing repeat takes that would make a scenario seem real. Doillon was captivated because she allowed herself to seem like a real madwoman, and she was believable at it. And Birkin basked in his gaze. She had always been typecast as either sunny or seductive. Doillon could see who she really was, not what she projected to the outside world. She was someone who, since childhood, had had a lot of sadness that she hid and felt shame about rather than try to resolve where it came from and why. He saw how her dark side made her more compelling as a person, and as an actress, and encouraged her to bring it to life. He was the kind of director who liked to make small suggestions for each take, and she was a good listener who took his direction well. Birkin gave some of the credit to Doillon, whom she described as an actor's director. He was patient, known to do dozens of takes of a scene until he got the perfect emotional response. "I knew that if I jumped, he would be there to receive me. He wouldn't opt for anything less," she said.

His presence allowed for a sort of escape from her life as a starlet and tabloid figure and a vision of freedom, even if it was cursory. She had filmed the part of Anne at the tail end of her relationship with Gainsbourg. She was at a tender juncture in her life, and the tortured character was an outlet. In the role, she finally channeled that melancholia onscreen that she wrote about so frequently in her diaries. By giving the audience a window into her pain, she allowed them to see her in a new light—as a real artist.

The Prodigal Daughter was also the first time viewers saw Birkin have a total disregard for vanity. Her presence—and quite literally her physicality—was changed for the role. Doillon and the costume designer Mic Cheminal had the idea that Birkin should look different from the woman who wore hot pants and regularly appeared in couture in *Vogue*; he wanted to downplay her innate glamour for the film. So she grew out her signature bangs and her hair, often wearing it swept back in a low bun. Cheminal styled her character in tailored clothes like trousers and blazers and a shirt primly buttoned all the way to the neck. Anne, in her state of melancholy, wears no makeup; the viewer sees that, in her early thirties, Birkin's face has hollowed out a bit with age, looking more angular. It's the first time onscreen that she really looks like an adult. In 2017, during a retrospective of her work at the Cinemathèque Française, Birkin said that in *The Prodigal Daughter* "I felt like I suddenly looked like myself." All the erotic power she had in previous films as a comedic character or a nymphet had been flattening. *This* was the real her.

Birkin's aesthetic offscreen evolved during this era too. She started wearing clothes that mirrored her *Prodigal Daughter* wardrobe: baggy trousers and oversize tanks, much of it from men's departments. The Mary Janes that had been a staple of her look were swapped out for tennis shoes, sometimes worn without laces for ultimate ease. Even the way she dressed for red carpets and black-tie events changed. She thought she looked ropy in cocktail dresses, so when she dressed up, she began to wear tuxedos. In press photos from this era, she looks both slinky and comfortable, exuding ultimate confidence in her body.

When *The Prodigal Daughter* was released in 1981, it marked the key turning point in Birkin's creative evolution and the role that finally allowed her to see herself as a serious actress, the hints of her acting prowess, and what she had wanted while filming *La piscine* back in 1968 finally fulfilled. Maybe audiences were wrong about Birkin's talent all along, and maybe they were wrong about Birkin entirely. She was not a perky girl anymore, but rather someone whose natural beauty and easygoing nature made it all too easy to forget her nuance. She had aged into an actor who could show the melancholy and anxiety and insecurity she'd always had within her.

The press run for the film in the spring of 1981 followed suit in acknowledging what *Première* magazine called "The New Jane," the title of a profile praising her for finally breaking away from her woman-child character in favor of a persona that was mature and accomplished. "Jane Birkin Starts a New Life," *Le Soir Illustré* declared on its cover. *Elle* wrote that she was learning to smile again alongside photos of her walking with Doillon and carrying firewood at a country house.

Birkin continued her creative renaissance with another movie with Doillon, *The Pirate*, which was released in 1984. It was another absorbing shoot, with a lot of dialogue to learn, and the bar she set for herself was high—she wanted to be at least as well regarded as she was for *The Prodigal Daughter*. Birkin plays Alma, a married woman visited by her ex-lover Carole (Maruschka Detmers). Alma allows Carole to abduct her and take her to a hotel where she's pursued by a nameless friend of Carole's who happens to be a precocious child of around middle-school age (Laure Marsac). It's a noirish, psychological melodrama about people haunted by love that's moved less by plot than by emotion. The movie is one of Doillon's lesser films in terms of critical regard, but its performances are searing—especially the highly charged Birkin, who excels at showcasing her descent into emotional violence. "I was waiting for a role like *The Pirate* for years, but my face didn't match it," Birkin said. The *New York Times* critic Elisabeth Vincentelli wrote that her performance "felt like a new Jane Birkin, inhabiting her physicality in a way that was almost dangerously unrestrained."

There are nude scenes that put Birkin in a role reversal from her past roles as the sexually charged younger woman. This time she's playing against younger lover Carole, whose own body is lush and more voluptuous. Birkin as Alma, on the other hand, has a certain severity that is emphasized through her costuming: pencil skirts and pumps and a choppy bob haircut.

In a fascinating casting decision, Birkin's own brother Andrew played her character Alma's husband. He, comparatively, wasn't received well. He reported to his sister that at a critics' screening of the film he was booed whenever he appeared onscreen. She asked him jokingly if he was swimming back to England yet.

Birkin was again praised for her performance in *The Pirate*. It led to further parts—Patrice Chéreau, a famed theater director, saw a screening of the film and got the idea to offer her a role onstage in Marivaux's *La fausse suivante* (*The False Servant*). *The Pirate* also earned her the first of three César Award nominations, the French equivalent to the Oscars. On the night of the Césars, she arrived with her hair in a long bob, a diamond rivière necklace around her neck. In photos she looks confident and, despite being in a black gown with a plunging neckline, casual, or at least more comfortable with herself.

She did not win that night, but it was still a triumph. Birkin had found her purpose. The world was taking her more seriously, and she was finding her own artistic voice—even if it was still located in collaboration with another lover. Her success as an artist was a reflection of the change in the way she treated herself. She was making her fulfillment a priority, showing up with gravity in her own life and destiny, and taking charge of who she was as an actor, as a mother, and as a woman. She was moving on. Serge Gainsbourg still lived with a poster of Stanley Kubrick's film *Lolita* on his wall, but Jane Birkin had left him and abandoned her own Lolita years.

CHAPTER ELEVEN

A Newborn, a Schoolgirl, and a Teen

Jane Birkin spent much of 1982 hiding from paparazzi. Though she and Serge Gainsbourg had been apart for two years, she had heard he still collected press clippings of her. She didn't want to hurt him, and she wanted to be the one to break the news to him first: She was pregnant. In June, a day before the French celebration for Mother's Day, she told him she was expecting a baby with Jacques Doillon. "He took it so well yesterday," she wrote. "But today his voice is sad and low."

Birkin fell in love with Doillon with the same adolescent intensity she had with Gainsbourg and John Barry. Or at least that's the way she expressed it in her diaries. He was not just an escape from Gainsbourg, but a new obsession. "I wish I was twelve and had met him for the first time," she wrote of Doillon in 1981 while they were on vacation in Senegal. "And he'd be the first, maybe not the last but the first."

Even if she allowed herself private moments of reverie around her new love, she had a more mature approach to this relationship. She saw Doillon not as someone who needed her for inspiration or because he hated to be alone, but as a complex, imperfect person. That didn't mean their personalities always jelled. Doillon was yet another man in her life who was preternaturally sure of himself. He didn't like all the English spoken around her and couldn't stop organizing things or criticizing her natural level of clutter. "It was like going into a monastery; Jacques didn't drink or smoke. It was so nice for the children to set off with their bikes to the Bois de Boulogne, quite a different sort of life," Birkin said. But it also marked the end of a previous lifestyle she had really loved. "I could hardly believe on New Year's Eve we weren't going to go out to Maxim's to throw confetti at the waiters, but just sit, watching the clock until it was midnight. It was so still." Leaving Gainsbourg hadn't signaled the end of tempestuous relationships for her. Rather, in Doillon, she found another variation. She might have escaped blowout fights along the Seine but she was with yet another man who was fastidious and grumpy.

Linda Birkin said her sister's relationship with Doillon suffered because she wanted so much attention from her lovers. Jane never could understand why Doillon wasn't consumed with jealousy over Gainsbourg; she was certainly jealous where Doillon was concerned. Despite how well they worked together, or maybe because of the vulnerability it brought out, Birkin was plagued by nagging doubts about their relationship. The actress Juliette Binoche, who was in Doillon's 1985 film *Family Life* (a character that Doillon wrote based on Birkin's daughter Kate Barry), first met Birkin through him. "She was lovely, very kind of innocent and a little insecure," she said of Birkin. Birkin was jealous of all the actresses he worked with, who she imagined in her bleakest moments were all young, sexy, and in possession of a large chest. In her journals, she worried it would be a repeat of her relationship with John Barry, that he would leave her because she was too needy. Her fear was a projection of her own desires—because she often did think about packing her suitcases and going, she wrote in 1983.

Birkin and Doillon's daughter, Lou Doillon, was born on September 4, 1982, calm to the point of scaring her parents because she cried so little in the first minutes of her life. Jacques Doillon was at Birkin's side for the birth, her first time doing it in Paris. Lou was an easy baby, and they liked that they could take her out to lunch at Angelina on rue de Rivoli, or for a quick escape abroad. Three weeks after giving birth, they took Lou to Italy with them so Birkin could present an award to Doillon at a film festival in Naples. Birkin may have grown beyond her years of bringing infants to nightclubs, but she would still indoctrinate Lou into her jet-setting lifestyle from birth.

After Birkin called Gainsbourg to tell him about the baby, he sent over a package with baby clothes and a card that read "Papa deux" ("Papa Two"), which remained his nickname with Lou, who was his goddaughter. He and Birkin kept in close proximity both emotionally and physically. "He was so essential in our lives. I always felt I had a metaphorical room in his house, and he had a very real room in our house, if he wanted it, with Charlotte there. I was proud of the relationship," Birkin said in 2007.

Birkin stayed close to Serge Gainsbourg after their breakup in 1980. She had divided her life so much into pre- and post-Gainsbourg that she called her diaries from after their separation *Post-Scriptum*, to mark the start of another life. It had the effect of sounding like everything that happened after her relationship with Gainsbourg ended was a footnote. Even though she never did go back to him, she allowed herself to pine for him. As the cliché goes, she found him both hard to live with and hard to live without—at least, based on an idealized version of their relationship. In 1981 she wrote, "I would like to be able to be with him again, a single day, at the best moment in our history, when I was certain that he would be mine forever. What was it like?" Even though she had been ready, even eager, to leave the relationship, the experience had been like leaving a family home, and they remained entwined.

Birkin was in a partnership that was still new while simultaneously parenting a newborn, a schoolgirl, and a teen, all in vastly different life stages with vastly different needs their mother had to meet. Life with Birkin's oldest daughter, Kate, was stormy. At first it seemed like typical adolescent issues: loud disagreements, exerting her own desire for independence. "She is hysterical like me, a little too much, better hearted than me, not resentful and devoured by jealousy like I was, but beautiful as I have never been and very desirable, I imagine," she wrote.

Birkin had set a confusing precedent around nightlife with her eldest daughter. When Kate turned twelve, her mother took her to the club Raspoutine at midnight to celebrate. Kate was thirteen when Birkin left Gainsbourg, the only father she had known, for Doillon. Now, in 1982, in a new relationship and with a new baby, Birkin didn't go out at night nearly as much, so when fifteen-year-old Kate rebelled, her mother noticed it. During Kate's teenage years, she had a habit of sneaking out of the house via a bedroom window. She went to nightclubs with her girlfriends and argued with her mother over whether she'd stolen her clothes. Birkin did not like conflict; she just wanted to keep the peace at home.

Doillon and Kate had a particularly fraught relationship as stepfather figure and daughter. In 1982, Doillon accused her of taking his tuxedo jacket, which had been missing for two weeks. Kate insisted that she had never seen it, and besides, she didn't have any particular use for a man's jacket. Doillon wouldn't let it go and went hunting through the house for it but never found it. Two weeks later, it appeared in his closet. Birkin was about to accuse him of making a big deal of something that had been in plain sight all along when he pointed out that there were smears from foundation on the lapel, blond hair on the collar, and a tube of lipstick left in a pocket. Kate didn't apologize or take any real responsibility for what had happened, instead saying that he had the wrong idea and that she had lent the jacket to a friend. He was pale with rage. Stealing became a habit: Birkin's Yves Saint Laurent jacket, a black dress made personally by Monsieur Saint Laurent, a cashmere sweater, and Repetto swimsuits all went missing, only to resurface in Kate's room. Perhaps she was working out some of the drama of having a beautiful and legendarily well-dressed mother with expectations that, as her daughter, she would effortlessly follow in her footsteps.

Those are the all-too-normal hardships of a blended family and of raising teenagers. John Barry, Kate's father, who'd been largely absent from the day-to-day child-rearing and was living in the United States, took on a slightly larger role in his daughter's life during her teen years. "What's he got to lose? A beautiful daughter, teenager, who really he couldn't be bothered to send a Christmas card to for twelve years," Birkin wrote in her journal in 1980, when Kate was thirteen. "But what can I do if Kate wants to see him? I can't stop her."

In the summer of 1982, Kate left for a month to visit her father. Birkin spent a month in peace without teenage screaming or crying. But when Kate came back to France, more trouble ensued. Her grades were so poor, she had to repeat a grade, and her antics outside the home were getting wilder, edging beyond standard-grade teenage rebellion into more concerning behavior, verging on substance abuse. One night she told her mother she was having a friend over early for dinner while Birkin went out to a nightclub. Birkin was ordering a Coca-Cola for herself and champagne for a friend when she saw Kate at a table across the room, holding court with six or seven other people. Birkin walked over, dragged her fifteen-year-old daughter outside, and spanked her on the rear for the first time in a decade right in front of an usher, who said, "Oh, Kate, you're leaving early!"

When Barry turned sixteen in 1983, Birkin wrote her a letter acknowledging that she had let her loose in a world of adults with a nonexistent father and an imposing stepfather (she seemed to have meant Gainsbourg, but it could have been Doillon as well), admitting that she had been a selfish mother. She hoped her daughter was merely in her chrysalis phase and that soon she'd rid herself of what was holding her back to become a butterfly. Birkin didn't want to actually deal—or was simply incapable of dealing—with her daughter's real problems, and, as a result, Kate's behavior spun out of control. Years later, in 2005, Kate had an art show and wrote about that time in her life in an essay. "I went into a tailspin as a teenager because there was no longer any authority at home. We spiral out of control, we look for a refuge, somewhere to wrap ourselves, around whom to wrap ourselves," she wrote. "I helped myself as best I could. I found different refuges. With lovers, in my work, but also in drinks and other less legal substances."

After years of having almost no involvement in his daughter's life, John Barry would have Kate visit him in the United States or see her in Europe. Birkin made an effort to put her feelings about her estranged ex-husband aside long enough to call him with updates on how their daughter appeared to be faring with her education and whether she was still sneaking out.

In 1986, John and his wife, Laurie, called Birkin and told her that they could tell Kate had been taking drugs and wanted her to go to treatment. Barry's wife, who was twenty-four years younger than John and had helped him get sober after they married in the late '70s, could be heard, Birkin wrote in her journal, yelling in the background that Yves Saint Laurent was on drugs and that Birkin's Paris crowd was a world of drug addicts. Laurie suspected Kate was using cocaine as her drug of choice.

Discipline was not Jane's forte as a mother; she felt she lacked the courage to displease her children. Birkin wanted her daughter to stay in design school in Paris to further her education and finish a final fashion collection for her own morale. She figured Kate could put off her addiction and deal with drinking and drugs after graduation. Plus, if her father was so concerned, Birkin said, then surely he would be more than willing to fly out and see her in person. But, no, he told her he was working on a movie and would possibly be free in six weeks.

Kate's problems continued to escalate. In February 1986, Barry and her boyfriend, Pascal, were arrested for drugs and went to jail overnight. While waiting for her arraignment the following day, Birkin wrote Kate a letter as Charlotte sobbed in the room, saying she was torn between wanting to scold her and wanting to hold her. Birkin recounts in the letter that she wanted to visit Barry after hours in jail, possibly pulling some strings to make it happen, but was confronted by a woman working there who said celebrities didn't have any special privileges over any other distraught mothers. "I considered myself different," she wrote in her diary. It was just a moment of reflection on her treatment versus anyone else's. She was focused entirely, myopically, on her own family life. Later that year, Kate went to a rehab clinic in England that followed the practices of Narcotics Anonymous and Alcoholics Anonymous.

In the mid-'80s, while her sister Kate's addiction was escalating, Charlotte Gainsbourg was, by contrast, becoming a star in her own right. It was an aspiration she'd had from an early age. When she was around ten, Charlotte was asked what she wanted to do for a living. "I want to be an actress like my mother and a drunkard like my father," she replied. Charlotte was known as the sensitive and anxious one in the family. She also had a dry sense of humor; even so, it was a particularly dark joke for a ten-year-old to make. Then again, Charlotte had been inundated with the world's loud opinions about her parents her whole life. Maybe she was lashing out. "I heard monstrosities about him growing up," Charlotte Gainsbourg said of her father in *Vanity Fair*. "That he was a drug addict, which he wasn't—he was an alcoholic and a great smoker, but no drugs. That my mother was a whore because she posed naked on magazine covers." That did not prevent her from wanting to follow them into the same fields.

In 1983, a casting director told Birkin and Doillon she was looking for a little boy to be in a movie about a divorce starring Catherine Deneuve. Birkin asked her, "Could this little boy be a girl, and when she smiles you feel like crying?" The director said yes. "So I said, 'Well, she's at home. Look no further.'" When Birkin got back, she left a note for twelve-year-old Charlotte on the kitchen table telling her there were screen tests for a film happening nearby and she should give it a try.

All the time Charlotte had spent watching VHS tapes with her father or on set with her mother paid off. She got the part in the film, which was called *Paroles et musique* (*Music and Lyrics*), a musical rom-com about a newly single A&R rep (Catherine Deneuve), a new act she's working with, and her estranged American husband. Gainsbourg plays a wise-beyond-her-years daughter who steals every scene she is in. Birkin approved of Charlotte going into film, particularly in light of Kate's own trouble. "I always thought that it was safer to be an actress at twelve than to be a lonely teenager at twelve and try to get into nightclubs," she said. The movie got mixed reviews, with many saying the script lacked focus. But Charlotte was ready for her next role. She was Parisian royalty as the daughter of Birkin and Gainsbourg. She seemed primed for the public eye and thrived in it.

The director Claude Miller saw Charlotte's debut and cast her as the lead in his next film, a coming-of-age movie called *L'effrontée* (*An Impudent Girl*). He was impressed with her acting but also thought casting her would give his film some built-in publicity. "Charlotte was in a way already a star because of her parents—people went to see her out of curiosity," he said.

Charlotte played a thirteen-year-old named Charlotte, but that was where the similarities between her life and her character's ended. Her character is a rather caustic working-class tomboy in provincial France who lives with her widower father and her brother. Her sole friend is a younger girl named Lulu, who Charlotte thinks is a bit of a pest. She meets Clara, a piano prodigy, which gives her a glimpse into a different way of life. The themes around class and growing up and wanting to escape the town you're stuck in are well trod, but Charlotte, like her mother, brings a naturalism to her role—not a hint of cloying child star. Instead, she's cynical; she seems unusually wise but emotionally fragile at the same time. Her own naturally androgynous looks, with short hair sticking out in every direction, just add to the feeling of being stuck in a place and a body.

When the film was released in 1985, it became a hit in France. Charlotte's performance was so acclaimed, she was nominated, at fourteen years old, for Most Promising Actress at the February 1986 César Awards. Serge Gainsbourg took his daughter (who looked adorable in a suit from the quintessentially French designer agnès b.) and Birkin to the awards in a Rolls-Royce rented for the occasion. He was drunk and swiped a bottle of champagne as soon as they arrived, hiding it under his chair and loudly joking that he was going to beat the shit out of all the other nominees if his daughter didn't win. Luckily for them, and maybe for Gainsbourg, she did win. When she tried to make a speech, she started crying, purely from being overwhelmed by the emotions of the moment. Birkin wrote that she was overjoyed that her daughter had won, and she was relieved that Gainsbourg hadn't made more of a fool of himself.

After the ceremony, Birkin, Charlotte, and Serge went to dinner at the restaurant Jules Verne, located in the Eiffel Tower, to celebrate. Just before dinner, eighteen-year-old Kate joined them. First she had to make an announcement: She was pregnant. She joked that she was making a boyfriend for her baby sister Lou. Birkin wasn't quite ready for humor; she was stunned by the news. She was going to be a grandmother at the age of thirty-nine. Birkin was an understanding parent, and she was in a position to know what Kate was going through better than many mothers—she'd also had Kate very young. If Birkin had wanted to spend the rest of the night focused on Charlotte's success, it was impossible. Both Birkin and Gainsbourg wondered aloud if Kate's boyfriend was going to prison, and her response was that she would just marry him in a prison uniform, then. She got up and headed for the exit, breaking glasses in her wake.

Charlotte's star continued to rise. At the same time she began her acting career, she also began to make music with her father, in a way that echoed some of the scandalous collaborations of her parents. At the age of thirteen, Charlotte recorded a duet with her father called "Lemon Incest," which he said was a pun on how the phrase "lemon zest" sounded with a French accent. The lyrics were not particularly subtle, with Charlotte singing about a love that was rare and off-limits and her father calling her his flesh and blood. In a sense she was reprising her mother's role in the song "Je t'aime . . . moi non plus." "Lemon Incest" was a massive hit in France. It debuted on October 27, 1985, at number four on the French charts, climbed to number two the next week, and spent fourteen weeks on the charts, ten of them in the top ten.

Jane Birkin spoke about the song many times over the years and generally called it a father-daughter love song and praised it in a breezy way. "I think the point with 'Lemon Incest' was that he wanted to put Charlotte on a pedestal, but he was a very shy man. He could never take anyone in his arms like some fathers do," she said in 2020. "His way of saying things was to write as beautiful a song as he could about how he loved her. He couldn't resist the temptation of making a pun between 'incest' and 'zest.' He knew perfectly well that it would shock people but that was secondary, in a way."

The video only added to the shock value. The two of them were filmed in bed together. Gainsbourg was bare-chested and wearing jeans, and Charlotte wore panties and a shirt. At the time, Charlotte insisted she loved the song, but much later she admitted discomfort: "I look at it now and I see how uncomfortable I look in the video, like a robot."

In a 2016 interview she said that, at the time, "I understood the subject. And it seemed normal to me . . . that people have desires." Upon further reflection, in her mid-forties, she maintained she still didn't take issue with her song or her father asking her to sing it. "Incest is so shocking and so taboo. It's as if he was amusing himself with that," she said. "But when you listen to the lyrics, he's just talking about the infinite love of a father for his daughter and of a daughter for her father—and you can't condemn that. Because there's nothing physical. So, yes, he *says* incest, but that's it. I find it terrible that you can't talk about things that are . . . [She pauses.] You hear the word 'incest' and conversation gets shut off. There's no dialogue."

The song was not Charlotte Gainsbourg's only foray into the taboo subject. In 1986, Serge Gainsbourg directed her in a film about incest called *Charlotte for Ever*. (Her career was so steeped in what was autobiographical and what wasn't that, by age fourteen, this was the third character she had played named Charlotte.) Then, in 1993, Charlotte Gainsbourg was cast in her first English-language role, an adaptation of Ian McEwan's *The Cement Garden*, a sort of highbrow variation of *Flowers in the Attic* in which Gainsbourg was the older sister in an incestuous relationship. The film was directed by her uncle, Andrew Birkin.

The concept of *épater la bourgeoisie*—to shock the respectable bourgeois class—has a long history in France. Rooted in the work of nineteenth-century romantic poets like Arthur Rimbuad and Charles Baudelaire, it was also a favorite trope of the Surrealists and Dadaists fifty years later—playing with themes of drugs or sex or societal taboos. Serge Gainsbourg was arguably loosely working in the same tradition, whether his art seemed deranged or inspired. Taken in the context of his public history of provocation, "Lemon Incest" seems to be another attempt to court shock value in his art and another way for an aging man to bring attention to himself.

The song was scandalous, but in France it had some context. "Lemon Incest" was just the latest manifestation of Gainsbourg's ever-escalating persona of the chaotic brute who lived to offend. He called this character, this Mr. Hyde version of himself, "Gainsbarre." His boorish behavior continued to escalate into new and offensive realms. He recorded a reggae version of "La Marseillaise," the national anthem, that was decried, and, most infamously, in 1986 he harassed the singer Whitney Houston on a French talk show, touching her hair, invading her personal space, and declaring in English, "I want to fuck her."

If Charlotte was inured to the blowback from "Lemon Incest," she couldn't shield herself from everything her parents did. In 1987, Gainsbourg burned a 500-franc note (worth roughly $100 at the time) on live television to show how little money he had left after taxes. It was illegal to do and a pompous way to make a statement. Charlotte, who seemed to be developing into an introvert, with a voice that was even more soft-spoken and breathy than her mother's, bore some of the brunt of this stunt. At school, some bullies approached her, stole her homework, and burned it to mimic her father burning cash.

In 1987, when Charlotte was sixteen, she came home from school one afternoon to find an upset-looking Birkin surrounded by the police. The police officers explained to Charlotte that she had been the target of a plot by fellow upper-class teenagers to kidnap her. In the press they were called the *blousons dorés*, golden jackets, gangsters who had already committed a few armed robberies. The gang had now concocted a more violent plan: First they intended to kill a member of the police in order to steal his uniform. (They were so serious that they had bought shovels to bury him.) Then someone would don the uniform, abduct Charlotte Gainsbourg, and stash her away in a country house. They would then ask for a ransom of 5 million francs, which was roughly equal to $1 million.

Charlotte would later play down the whole episode as amusing and ridiculous and laugh about it, but her parents were terrified for her safety. Serge Gainsbourg made her go to school accompanied by a bodyguard for a while; then her parents took safeguarding her to another level and decided to send her to the Collège Alpin International Beau Soleil, a boarding school in Switzerland that counts a Danish princess and three princes of Luxembourg as fellow alumni. Charlotte was safe, but Birkin's nerves were frayed.

Birkin was a mother trying her best, or at least her own version of that. In the second half of the 1980s, as she was entering middle age, her life mirrored those of other women of her generation, dealing with divorces and blended families and career highs and lows. But on closer inspection, that life resembled the trappings of a European drama about an unconventional family: She had a loutish ex whose own addictions were catching up with him; one overachieving daughter, a child star; another daughter who was an addict with a child on the way; and a baby to care for. Birkin's reality was far beyond the tabloid coverage of her or the film roles she took on. And that's the part of Birkin's life as a middle-aged woman that no profusion of images of her in hot pants and boots can ever capture.

CHAPTER TWELVE

The Me and the I

In 1985, Jane Birkin wrote a short note to the Belgian-born director Agnès Varda, arguably the best-known woman to come out of the French New Wave cinema. In it, she detailed how much she enjoyed Varda's latest film, *Sans toit ni loi* (literally "without a roof or rule," although the English title is *Vagabond*). The movie's protagonist, a young woman named Mona, wanders through French wine country during winter and has a series of encounters with locals. *Vagabond* is filmed almost like a documentary, with its somber characters and naturalistic acting. Its impact derives not from plot mechanics but from how it has steeped in humanity, sometimes coming off as grim, sometimes silly. Varda might have been surprised that a film about being alone had resonated so deeply with Birkin, except she couldn't decipher Birkin's handwriting ("illegible" and "chicken scratch" were the descriptors she used), so she called her up and asked if they could get together.

The two went on a walk in the Parc de Sceaux in the Paris suburbs. Varda told Birkin she had an idea for her next film, but it was still just a sketch: something about seasons—the passing of time—that didn't resemble a classic feature film. Birkin, who was on the verge of turning forty, told her she had been thinking quite a bit about aging and that it scared her. She worried that maybe one day she'd just be sitting on a bench like the ones they were walking by, no more important than a dead leaf on the ground. Varda, meanwhile, had the vantage point of being nearly twenty years her senior.

She thought forty was when a woman came into her own personally and artistically. This juncture in her life was the ideal time to portray Birkin on film.

After that conversation, Birkin and Varda embarked on an artistic run together that brought new texture to Birkin's legacy. Birkin instigated the collaboration, taking control over her creative expression and showing more agency over her career than she had ever before exerted. Agnès Varda specifically was important too. While Birkin had landed well-regarded roles with auteurs like her partner Jacques Doillon, taking on a role without masculine oversight was a new direction for her.

Jane B. par Agnès V., a documentary that coincided with Birkin turning forty in 1986, sought to create a filmic environment that showed Jane Birkin outside of how the world had previously viewed her, loosely exploring both how Varda saw her and how Birkin saw herself. To film it, Varda set up cameras in Birkin's cozy home on rue de la Tour in the 16th arrondissement for a year and observed her in her natural habitat. Birkin likened it to living together. The result is something intimate, fresh, and undeniably female.

Watching it occasionally feels like sitting in on a session of psychoanalysis on film, exploring Birkin's fantasies, desires, insecurities. Varda abandons any pretense of traditional format. There are neither talking heads commenting on Birkin, nor re-creations of her life, nor any kind of linear storytelling about her background. "I was trying to invent a new category," Varda said. "I was asking, what is an actress? How can she be herself?"

The film begins with an anecdote from Birkin in which she relays how she once threw up after drinking sherry alone on her birthday a decade before and looked into a mirror afterward, declaring, "Shit, this is thirty." She's telling it while dressed as a Renaissance noblewoman, which gives an indication of the surreal, fanciful, and diaristic tone of the documentary, blending scenarios of reality with farce.

Throughout the documentary, Birkin appears as different female characters in non sequitur fantasy skits. Some of them are the types of roles for which she was overlooked for appearance, age, accent, acting style: Joan of Arc, Calamity Jane, Tarzan's Jane. At one zany point, she plays Stan Laurel of Laurel and Hardy (Varda plays Oliver Hardy). Other sequences are less specific and more representative of general female archetypes: posed like a nude odalisque in an Ingres painting; costumed as a flamenco dancer complete with fan and ruffled skirt and doing a little dance. The montages of Birkin showing up in female drag give the film a surrealist texture, with the insight of a tarot reading in which Birkin is the different cards and Varda the interpreter of them.

It was Agnès Varda's idea to include Birkin as renditions of artworks and characters, which caused some friction—Birkin felt like Varda's toy. "The people I loved in my life were authoritarian in their love for me," she told *Marie Claire* of her relationship with collaborators. "I'm used to others having better ideas than me and being a bit bossy." She trusted Varda and the project enough to be fully in her hands, even if she said she felt self-conscious decked out flamenco-style. At forty, she was ready to go beyond her comfort zone; with Varda, she could let go and try anything.

The fantasy sequences are amusing and look lush, but the film is strongest when it's documenting Birkin and Varda relating as two middle-aged women about their real lives in a conversation about what it is to be a woman moving through the world. While Birkin is the ostensible subject, Varda frequently appears in the frame, so *Jane B. par Agnès V.* is a film nearly as much about Varda as about Birkin. It is an exploration of the female gaze, which Birkin had never put herself under—something she may even have avoided up until then.

At one point Varda notes that Birkin rarely looks into the camera in photos; Birkin responds that it is too personal to do so. And yet she allows herself to be fully taken in by Varda's camera, which lingers over parted lips, her nipple, her eyes, as a woman in possession of great beauty. She is just as naked as she was when posing in a pornography magazine or moaning false orgasms for "Je t'aime . . . moi non plus" with Gainsbourg, and she is in on her own objectification because, in this documentary, it is just one of many incarnations. She also shows up onscreen the way she sees herself day-to-day, in denim and a sweater, talking in a café about her three daughters.

Jane B. par Agnès V. is effective at making Birkin seem like a real person beyond an image or part of a relationship. At age forty, Birkin had a rich understanding of her own psychology, especially around stardom. She wanted everyone to like her, but she also craved anonymity, two things that were maybe not in opposition to each other but not complementary. "I'm still here," she says in the film. "You're watching me as time passed."

Birkin was set to make her live concert debut in March 1987, almost twenty years after she started performing onstage professionally, at the Bataclan in Paris. It had been her agent's idea. He asked if she wanted to sing—and not lip-sync, as she always had before—in a grand concert hall. She was noncommittal, saying maybe one day she would like to. "This might be your last chance," he responded. She found that mildly offensive but agreed to it. Agnès Varda, who was embedded with Birkin working on their documentary project, would film it.

A few nights before the concert, Serge Gainsbourg asked her what kind of dress she was going to wear. She shook her head, saying she wasn't planning on wearing a dress but rather something more masculine, like a men's coat. "But you'll do your hair with curls in it?" he countered. That wasn't part of the plan either. Instead, she borrowed a pair of nail scissors from him and got to it, shaping her hair into a pixie. She wanted the audience at the Bataclan to focus on the lyrics she sang rather than her appearance. It was an act of abandoning her girlhood; by doing it, she also looked less classically pretty. To debut the haircut at the solo concert was a way of defying Gainsbourg's perception of her—and the public's. She would still be singing songs written for her by her ex, such as "Jane B." and "Di doo dah," but asserting her artistic growth in other ways. "So, no, I wasn't going to swing my hair around like Serge wanted me to or lick my lips, which is what he thought I should do. Because that was the person he had known before. Such a Lolita, I didn't want to do that anymore," she said in 2016.

The night of the concert she ended up wearing a men's shirt and a white tank top tucked into white men's trousers accessorized with just a thin red belt and sneakers. Her friend Gabrielle Crawford watched her suffer from nerves all day: anxiety, hives, vomiting into a toilet in the greenroom. Onstage in Varda's film, singing "Le moi et le je" ("The Me and the I"), which is about the dichotomy of wanting to be seen and to be ignored, Birkin looks at ease, as if performing for an audience is an act of muscle memory—she had been doing it for more than half her lifetime—but unsure of how she will be received; this was an entirely new way of showing herself to her fans.

Gainsbourg wanted to be there, but he claimed he wanted to be unseen by fans—this was her night—so he came in right after the concert started and stood near the stage in the shadows. Except that the promise to be invisible wasn't one he could keep. Close to the end of her set, he stepped toward the light and lit a cigarette, fully illuminating his face to the audience. He literally stole her spotlight. Birkin knew he'd pull something like that. To Crawford, who was standing with Gainsbourg that night, Birkin joked that at least he'd had the dignity to wait until the end of her show.

Both the solo show and the Varda documentary built on the sense that she was continuing on her creative trajectory. It was also a relatively quiet moment in terms of publicity. There was no glitzy premiere for the documentary as there had been for her earlier films such as *Slogan*. Mainstream French media took note of the latest Birkin chapter, but it wasn't the fanfare of years past. In April 1987, *Télé Loisirs* mentioned her triumph at the Bataclan, calling her the "ex-baby doll of the sixties" who still had a wild brand of charm. *TV Hebdo*, the French equivalent of *TV Guide*, noted the "shock" of her work with Varda in November 1988. She had lived in France for about two decades. The mere presence of Jane Birkin was no longer a novelty.

The next project between Birkin and Varda came immediately after *Jane B.* "It's lovely, at 40, to come across someone who loves you and wants to film you. I also guessed that Agnès saw herself through me, like Serge and Jacques ultimately," Birkin wrote. The two women teamed up to work on a script called *Kung Fu Master*, with Birkin doing the story and Varda writing the screenplay. *Kung Fu Master* is a feature film about an affair between a forty-year-old woman, Mary-Jane (Birkin), and one of her daughter's fifteen-year-old classmates, Julien. It's a premise that, like many of Birkin's roles, explored taboo behavior. "Though French films are often breezy and sophisticated about just this sort of sexual initiation, 'Kung Fu Master' has all the naïveté of a twelve-year-old girl addicted to romance novels and all the charm of her smelly gym socks," wrote a critic in the *New York Times*. Varda's gaze is neutral, as if forcing the viewer to make up their own mind about the relationship. Julien is obsessed with the arcade video game *Kung-Fu Master*, in which the titular protagonist must rescue a damsel in distress. The way Birkin plays Mary-Jane, the affair is less about her sexual passion for a teen than a way for a lonely woman to buy time and put off aging. We are to believe she is in love with Julien's innocence. The movie never makes it clear how far they take things sexually, but he is the one who makes the first move. The focus is on Mary-Jane's misplaced immaturity—she plays video games with Julien, and in one scene he suggests they meet in a hotel bar to celebrate getting his braces removed. Birkin and Varda could not resist an additional element of provocation in casting: The daughter was played by Charlotte Gainsbourg, who was turning fifteen the summer it was filmed, and Julien was played by Varda's own son Mathieu Demy, who was almost fourteen. "I don't see it as controversial," said Varda. "I see it as off-center." In his review, the critic Roger Ebert wrote, "What redeems this movie and allows it to work is that it is about feelings, not actions. The film really is about the phenomenon of the romantic crush—about how another person suddenly can seem to embody an ideal for us."

The two projects are unlikely sisters. Both represent creative breakthroughs for Birkin, each one something she had never shown to the public before. *Kung Fu Master* allowed her to try her hand at screenplays, and *Jane B. par Agnès V.* allowed her to embrace, bare, and skewer her image. Upon entering middle age, she was ready to dismantle her legacy as the muse.

There is a scene in the documentary just after she dumps out the contents of her handbag in which Varda, unseen, says that Birkin was revealed by the men who loved her—that they wrote songs and films for her. The camera leisurely pans over a pond covered in lily pads while a piano plays, until we come upon Birkin, dressed in diaphanous white clothes and a crown of flowers, standing against a tomb. She is supposed to be a literal muse in the mythological sense. "I was told muses never die," says Varda as Birkin walks around the tomb. "They pine away, but some die of boredom, let themselves go, wreck their hair color, bite their nails, and never sing again." Birkin says nothing; as we gaze at her, she looks right back at the camera without a flinch. When she starts to talk, she says that she spent years inspiring her poet. "Still, these weary muses, they know their job. They weep in eternal delight," says Birkin. "Me, I weep in anger."

This moment, however bathed in fantasy, is the closest Birkin has ever gotten to revealing herself. She's showing all her cards with Varda as her conspirator. She is painfully aware of her reputation as a perky, sexy sprite who is at her best when she's inspiring great men. She knows the power inherent in it and she knows she's also more than that. This is Birkin as her truest self, manipulating her own image. It turns out she was in on the joke all along.

CHAPTER THIRTEEN

Birkin Like the Bag

The story of the Birkin bag began as the ultimate serendipitous meet-cute. Jane Birkin was on an Air France flight to London from Paris in 1983 and had been upgraded to first class. The basket bag she carried, her signature since her London years, was in poor shape. Jacques Doillon had reversed his car over the bag a few days prior after a petty but nonetheless deeply felt argument, which he capped off by yelling, "It's terrible for you to be known for your object." As she boarded the plane, all her life's effects were falling out of it: wallet, keys, pens, business cards, diapers for Lou, cigarettes, glasses.

The man seated next to her eyed the scenario and suggested she should consider owning a bag with pockets. She sighed and told him that the day Hermès made one with pockets, that would be lovely and she would buy it. He responded that he *was* Hermès, so he could do exactly that.

The man in question was Jean-Louis Dumas, then the chief executive of Hermès and the sixth generation of family leadership in the most vaunted of French luxury houses. It is a name that rings with intimations of status: money (bags often sell for close to $15,000), scarcity (the bags are such a luxury that there are often waitlists to land one), and craftsmanship (each bag is assembled by a single person).

Hermès was founded in 1837 by Thierry Hermès, whose entire family died either during the Napoleonic Wars or from sicknesses.

He apprenticed making harnesses for sixteen years before becoming a master craftsman and opening a shop in Paris, where he specialized in saddles. As the nineteenth century turned into the twentieth and affluent customers were buying more cars than horses, Hermès diversified and began to use its craftsmen to make leather goods.

With cars and trains plus greater social mobility during the first few decades of the twentieth century, travel increased, and so did demand for high-quality leather goods. (For example, Louis Vuitton had built a fortune on trunks that were flat and ideally suited for train travel rather than traditional trunks with rounded tops that were designed for rain to roll off when they were stowed in the open atop carriages.) At the time they began to produce their leather goods, Hermès was unbranded, but those in the know understood the quality associated with the bags (an early harbinger of so-called quiet luxury, perhaps). The Hermès signature was—and remains—its saddle stitch, a technique where two needles pass over a single hole in a way that cannot be replicated by a machine.

In the 1950s, the company reached a new level of visibility, with pop culture and fashion colliding in a way that signaled the brand's preeminence. The American actress Grace Kelly was photographed in *Life* magazine leaving a building with her husband, holding her Hermès *sac à main de voyage*, a travel handbag, over her abdomen. The world would soon learn that she was trying to hide the fact that she was pregnant with her first daughter with Prince Rainier of Monaco. Hermès had designed the bag in 1935 but renamed it the Kelly bag after this legendary pairing was spotted. The Kelly became what is to this day a classic It Bag.

Though there was high demand for a Kelly, the Hermès customer base was still made up of a small coterie of the ultra-wealthy. There was not yet the push for mass-market luxury or even the idea of accessible luxury. But houses like Hermès and Louis Vuitton needed to produce popular bags because women, especially the younger generation, were buying fewer gloves and hats and evening bags. Department stores that once had large counters dedicated solely to evening gloves had scaled down such inventory. But a nice big handbag that could fit everything that women carried with them? Still an open market.

Birkin asked her seatmate why the company didn't yet make a handbag that was bigger than the Kelly but smaller and lighter than its Haut à Courroies, which her ex Serge Gainsbourg had carried for years. Dumas was intrigued, as Hermès was dealing with a generational crisis of how to evolve the company without losing its core customers. Proper, petit bourgeois adults sought out the Kelly and their other bags. And Queen Elizabeth II of England and lesser matrons were avid fans of the brand's printed silk scarves. But Hermès wasn't exactly cool in the eyes of baby boomers, who were starting to age into real spending power. With its orange boxes and quirky prints, Hermès could be seen as whimsical, but it was usually associated with uptight parents and grandparents.

Dumas asked Jane Birkin what her idea might look like. She got out the only paper she could find, which was an airsick bag in the seat back in front of her, and got to sketching a trapezoidal bag. It looked more casual than the Kelly, with two handles like a tote, and somewhat resembled a shrunken version of the Haut à Courroies Gainsbourg owned. Dumas said he would make one for her, though Birkin didn't think much about it.

A month later, Birkin was asked to come in and see a maquette, a prototype of the bag that a designer had constructed out of paper—akin to how a fashion designer might make a muslin version of a dress for fittings. She fiddled with it and went through leather samples and offered her opinion on which ones would be nice with the design.

The process of making an Hermès bag is notoriously laborious, to the point where the company claims a craftsperson should be able to see a bag on the street and recognize on sight whether they had personally made it. A Kelly bag could take around twenty hours, but the bag Birkin helped design was more complicated and took about forty hours to complete.

In 1984, Jane Birkin got another call from Hermès that her special-ordered bag was ready. Hermès has always prided itself on being a place where loyal customers with enough money can still place highly specific special orders with the lofty name Hermès Horizons: bespoke upholstery for a yacht, a knife holder for a chef, a crayon case for someone's kid, a baseball mitt. Birkin's bag was black box, a kind of calf leather, with gilded brass hardware, fashioned in a rectangular shape with saddle stitching and a burnished flap embossed with the initials JB. The bag was about sixteen inches high and eighteen inches wide and had a shoulder strap and, like the Kelly, a lock and key. And, importantly, it did indeed hold everything Birkin needed—useful *and* luxurious.

Dumas liked the bag Birkin had created enough that he wanted to make it part of their permanent collection, and to name the style after her—like the Kelly, but this would be the Birkin. "With pleasure," she responded. Hermès was not the only company to name bags after famous clients: Gucci made a Jackie bag after Jacqueline Kennedy Onassis, and Dior later named one for Princess Diana. The lauded French house of Hermès naming a bag after Birkin was claiming her for the French-speaking world the way they had claimed Grace Kelly after she moved to Monaco. It was a way of adopting her into the fold. Not that she gave up all her old British style traits—she still carried her basket bags, sometimes together with a Birkin if she had enough belongings to fill them both.

In naming the bag for her, Hermès was not asking her to model or endorse it. As a practice, Hermès did not—and to this day does not—do celebrity ad campaigns. Without that kind of splashy announcement, it often takes time for a product to take off, and the Birkin was no exception. The bag was also subtle for the mid-1980s, without overt logos or loud branding. And it was an investment, costing $2,000 ($6,000 adjusted for today's inflation). The Birkin intrigued the core Hermès customers, who lived in the tony 16th arrondissement, where Birkin herself lived, or on the equally tony Upper East Side in New York City. It was large enough to put in a planner (and, later, a laptop computer) and a big wallet and go to work, but it wasn't some anonymous leather tote; it was expensive and not easily purchased. That combination gave the bag enduring appeal.

The Birkin bag spread from denizens of wealthy neighborhoods to the world of celebrities, evolving from a much-desired accessory to a cultural touchpoint thanks to the scarcity market around it. Hermès didn't have to release sales figures of the Birkin, which created an additional layer of mystery: How many people were buying them? How many were even being made? Within about a decade of coming out, the Birkin was embraced by an array of celebrities, usually photographed with it held prominently on the forearm to prove that they could get their hands on one: from Carolyn Bessette-Kennedy and Melania Trump to Heidi Klum and Catherine Zeta-Jones to Lil' Kim and Beyoncé. The bag hit the larger zeitgeist when it became a plot point on *Gilmore Girls* and on *Sex and the City*, where in a 2001 episode public relations exec Samantha Jones uses the name of her client, the real-life actress Lucy Liu, to procure a Birkin for herself. When her ruse is discovered, she utters the memorable line: "It's not a bag, it's a Birkin!" A true statement if there ever was one.

Owning a Birkin was synonymous with making it. On NPR in 2015, Wednesday Martin, the author of *Primates of Park Avenue*, a book that took a wry anthropological view of the life of wealthy women, was a guest. She said that a woman she'd spotted striding the streets of Manhattan with a Birkin convinced her she needed one. "We were the only people on the sidewalk, and as she walked toward me, rather than keeping to the right, she was slowly but surely walking, sort of, at me so that I had to move further and further to the right," she said. "And I was ceding more and more sidewalk territory to her until, finally, I found myself stopping right up against this garbage can that she had sort of walked me into, then she brushed right by me with her handbag. That was a dominance display, and that woman used her handbag to do it. . . . That was the moment when I realized that handbags are really important in New York. And if I want to play ball on the Upper East Side, I better stop walking around with this white plastic bag with a couple of bananas in it. I better saddle up."

The Birkin was not a one-season sensation. It's a bag with a history and a proven track record. A 2024 article in *Fortune* pointed out that, since the value of a Birkin doubles about every five years, it is a superior investment to gold. But its overt luxury doesn't quite square with Jane Birkin's image. She was born into an upper-class family, but she wasn't an idle lady-who-lunches type. She fancied herself more of a hippie. In France they have a name for those children of

May '68 who wanted revolution and equality but also objects and wealth and entertainment and social status: *gauche caviar*, or caviar left, their equivalent of "champagne socialists" or "limousine liberals." Birkin embraced her namesake bag, but she did so in a way authentic to her and how she lived: carrying it everywhere as her everyday bag and cramming it with a Mary Poppins amount of stuff, including dog treats, expired prescriptions, Elizabeth Arden cream, and spare clothes, much as she had with her basket bags. Her friends deemed it a mobile warehouse, and Birkin said her bag weighed as much as a dead donkey. She let the bag get completely beat-up—not merely some scratches and patina from wear, but covered in stickers and key chains and with a nail clipper hanging off the handle. It made such a jangling sound that one could hear Birkin before seeing her approach. "Of course, that free feeling is why we love Jane Birkin and that Birkin specifically. She's in a moment wearing her item! Living her truth. Try bottling that to sell a product," wrote fashion journalist Liana Satenstein. "After all, we don't want the Birkin, we want Jane."

W. David Marx, the author of the book *Status and Culture*, said that for luxury goods to function as status symbols, they need cachet, an association with high-status lifestyles, and to be used in a way that is not only to mark status. Someone carrying a well-worn Hermès bag suggests that they are not wearing it simply because of its label, according to Marx. And you can see that in the way that the bag has entered into the pop culture realm: Candice Bergen's Instagram account is called Bergen Bags for her penchant for painting on Hermès. Mary-Kate Olsen owns a large Birkin so faded, it's no longer clear what color it is, black or green or blue. Julia Fox has a gray Birkin with slashes on its edges she claimed on TikTok were the result of a machete attack. These women are all in Jane Birkin's own lineage in carrying a precious bag and not being precious about it. That was her authentic way of wearing it.

Birkin herself was not a collector of the bag; she owned one at a time, mostly black, sometimes brown. She donated the very first Birkin to a charity auction for AIDS in 1994; its whereabouts were unknown for several years. That original Birkin was purchased by a woman named Catherine Benier, a collector who owns a jewel box of a boutique in Saint-Germain-des-Prés called Les 3 Marchés that sells rare Hermès and Chanel bags and accessories. Benier got a call in 2000 from an auction house in Paris that she needed to come see a bag as soon as possible. She arrived, and what emerged from the safe was the first-ever Birkin bag. "For me, it was extraordinary, like finding Adam's rib. It's the most beautiful, coveted piece in the history of fashion," she told the *New York Times*. In June 2025, she announced that she would be selling the bag on July 10, 2025, at an auction at Sotheby's in Paris. The original Birkin was anticipated to be among the most expensive bags, if not the most of, to sell at auction. "All these elements fuel the legend of the first Birkin bag, so certainly a price exists, but what is it?" Benier said. "This bag is the object of a lifetime, it's a legend, an icon. Does a legend have a price? Certainly." The bag sold to a Japanese collector for $10.1 million.

Birkin had a friendly relationship with the brand, often sitting in the front row of their shows near the Dumas family, her namesake bag at her feet. However, in 2015 she drew a line due to the company's ethics and threatened to boycott them and take her name off the bag over their use of exotic crocodile skins. "I have asked Hermès to debaptize the Birkin Croco until better practices in line with international norms can be put in place," she said in a statement. In reality, her action had no weight. The *New York Times* consulted Hugh Devlin, a lawyer at Withers LLP in London who specialized in the fashion sector, who said Hermès trademarked the name in 1997 and can thus use it as the company sees fit. Their solution was to no longer buy hunted skins but rather bring the farming in-house, use some for skin, and release other crocodiles into the wild. It was an imperfect compromise.

Jane Birkin had a total of five Birkin bags during her lifetime, including the prototype. She would occasionally sell one of her own bags to make cash donations to her pet causes, for her own humanitarian impact. She auctioned a retired Birkin bag in 2011 and donated the $163,000 it fetched to the victims of the Fukushima nuclear accident in Japan, a country that has always embraced her and where she is perhaps most popular after France.

Hermès made a fortune off Birkin's name, and she barely got any financial reward from it. Once Birkin saw how much Hermès was making off her namesake bag, she eventually convinced them to donate to her choice of charities. She spoke rarely about the agreement but did mention it in a 2011 interview with *Women's Wear Daily*, years before the crocodile incident. Hermès paid a reported $40,000 annually, but it's a paltry sum considering that is less than the retail cost of a few Birkins, and prices go up from there: In 2016, Christie's auction house set a world record for a rare matte white Himalaya Niloticus Diamond Birkin 30 with 18-karat white gold and diamond hardware; it sold for about $300,000.

Jane Birkin was never out to cash in on her name being on the bag; she treated the whole thing like an amusing accident. But having your name usurped by a handbag is a strangely dehumanizing experience. Once it became a hot item, Birkin was asked about the bag in seemingly every interview she sat for. She usually gave a wry and self-deprecating answer or just said that having a famous bag was a delight. If she resented the association, she never spoke about it publicly or to friends. Birkin was focused in the mid-1980s and '90s on growing into her own creatively; the Birkin bag was merely the result of a funny encounter in a life built on a series of funny encounters. She didn't attach much significance to the bag. That was something for everyone else—for those without namesake cachet and who were not lucky enough to float through life in the way that Birkin appeared to. She used the bag at times ironically, not as a status symbol—although that's not entirely true. The carefree way she used her Birkin was its own status symbol and class assertion, an inherent contradiction she never really rectified. Her behavior shows a carelessness about money—the kind of real money that could change a person's life. Birkin got her bags for free but she still carried them. That is how brands keep up the myth of luxury: that by owning a Birkin, you the wearer will belong and be understood to have somehow earned the privilege of owning it. Nor was there any moment when she lobbied hard to make real money off it. She was ultimately content to be its muse. The world desired the bag for the status associated with it; it increasingly had less to do with Birkin's imprint on it. Jane Birkin became more and more distantly associated with it until she became merely a fun fact about its inception.

This strange co-opting of her name can be best viewed by way of an encounter Birkin had while shopping in Istanbul. An enterprising carpet dealer tried to sell her a counterfeit Birkin, insisting his was superior to the one on her shoulder. “I already have one,” she said. “Mine is unique—it’s my bag.”

“I know, madame,” the carpet dealer replied. “There are plenty of them like that. They are imitations.” His, he noted, were better quality than all the others. Birkin would not let it go. “No, it’s the Birkin bag and I am the Birkin,” she said. The game of confused identity did not end until she got out her passport to prove who she was. The dealer wasn’t exactly starstruck. She didn’t end up buying a counterfeit bag, but she did let herself get wildly overcharged for a silk rug.

The Birkin bag solidified Birkin’s place in fashion history, but her name would never entirely belong to her again.

CHAPTER FOURTEEN

And You, Always

Jane Birkin contended onscreen with being an aging muse in *La belle noiseuse* (*The Beautiful Troublemaker*), filmed by the French director Jacques Rivette over the summer of 1990. The movie, which is a loose adaptation of an Honoré de Balzac short story, is a virtuosic four-hour-long examination of creativity and inspiration. *La belle noiseuse* is a kind of love triangle set in modern-day France involving a famous painter named Édouard Frenhofer (played by Michel Piccoli, Birkin's father in *The Prodigal Daughter* a decade before) and his younger wife, Liz (Birkin), who was the muse for the most notable years of his career.

Sometimes the dialogue sounds like it could have been pulled from Birkin's own diaries, even though she didn't write about the film at all in them. "At first he painted me because I loved him," she says in the film. "Then he painted me because he loved me." Before completing his last portrait of his wife, Frenhofer abandons it and retires from painting. That is, until he meets Marianne (Emmanuelle Béart), the girlfriend of a young artist, for whom he comes out of retirement.

Birkin has the less showy role of the aging muse whose portrait is literally painted over by her husband and replaced by Marianne. Marianne is portrayed as full of spunk and emotion; by contrast, Liz quietly pursues domestic tasks like baking while explaining away her husband's rudeness; she has to show that she believes in his creative potential more than her pride. Birkin elevates what could have been the thankless role of a jealous but ultimately supportive wife into something deeper—a true meditation on the nature of commitment and collaboration.

The film was the most lauded of Birkin's career. It won the Grand Prix at the Cannes Film Festival in 1991. The Japanese director Akira Kurosawa ranked it among his top one hundred films of all time. The American film critic Roger Ebert called it "the best film I have ever seen about the physical creation of art, and about the painful bond between an artist and his muse." Liz was a telling role for her to choose, given Birkin's own trajectory with John Barry, Serge Gainsbourg, and Jacques Doillon. She had begun the dismantling of her muse self with Agnès Varda and their documentary. Why stop now?

After their breakup in the early '80s, Gainsbourg continued to write songs for Birkin. The music's emotional tenor shifted with the end of their romance—what she inspired evolved along with their changing lives. In that sense their lyrics had taken a more substantive and satisfying turn as they aged. Their early collaborations, like the ones featured on the *Melody Nelson* album, were charming concoctions about a charming girl. Birkin loved them, but she was no longer that girl. Gainsbourg wrote a song called "Baby Lou" for Birkin's 1983 album *Baby Alone in Babylone*. That was their breakup album and proof, Birkin thought, that he also acknowledged her growth and respected her as an artist in her own right. She felt the music became richer. "There were songs that he wrote for me when we were together, songs that I see now were written for the baby doll, innocent sort of person he wanted me to be. And those songs were cute and sexy and flirtatious," she said in 2012. "But later in life, after I had left him, he continued to write songs for me and they were deeper. I felt I wasn't singing *me*, I was singing *him*. I was singing his feelings, his curiosity, his pain and difficulty in life."

In 1990, they recorded the album *Amours des feintes*. The recording was not going smoothly and her signature high notes weren't satisfying Gainsbourg. "I just tried to sing them as high as I could in pitch to make him as pleased as he could [be] and feel as if I was interpreting his words to the very highest of standards," she wrote in her journal.

Gainsbourg, who was sixty-one, was clearly exhausted throughout the recording process and in poor health. The year before, in 1989, he had undergone an operation on his liver, and he was having more heart trouble. She said there was no point in tiring himself out and recording so quickly, but he kept telling her he owed it to her.

As much as Jane Birkin moved ahead in her creative life in the 1980s, she frequently reverted to Gainsbourg for emotional support. They shared their daughter Charlotte, but it was a bond beyond that. She loved his parents and missed them. And no one, Birkin swore, could love him as much as she had—as she still did. "It's a lifetime of love for you, my darling. It's not about sleeping together, making love," she wrote in her diary after she left him in 1980. "You have my love forever, no matter how clumsy I am at expressing it."

After the Birkin-Gainsbourg relationship ended, he had almost immediately settled down with another woman—another very young woman, at that. Bambou was a twenty-year-old half-Chinese, half-German model-actress whose given name was Caroline Von Paulus. They met at the club that Gainsbourg, Birkin, and their set frequented, Élysée-Matignon. "Serge was everything to me," she told *Vanity Fair*. "He was my lover, my father—he was my real family." Gainsbourg and Bambou had a baby, Lucien, called Lulu, in 1986. Birkin felt like Gainsbourg had simply replaced her with a newer model of woman-child-muse. That could have been the only kind of woman who would put up with Gainsbourg at that point in his addictions. To her credit, Birkin never had a real rivalry with or laid her anger and resentment at Gainsbourg on his new girlfriend.

Instead, she and Gainsbourg were the kind of exes who still had dinner together at the Ritz and then went to the piano bar and then to yet another bar for cocktails. They would flirt a little over wine during these outings but mostly ruminate on their past in a way that was rather candid. "I was a bastard, I hit you," he told

Birkin, who recorded the conversation in her journal. She did not see herself as any kind of victim or battered wife. "No, no, not a bastard and I didn't care about being hit, it was indifference that killed me," she replied.

Their dynamic was not lost on Birkin's partner, Jacques Doillon. In 1990, to promote *Amours des feintes*, Birkin asked Gainsbourg to be her guest on a live TV show. She was asked, "What is Serge to you in one word?" She panicked and said the first word that popped into her mind: *toi*, you. "A stupid answer, but it was all I could think of," she wrote in her journal. The host asked Gainsbourg what Birkin was to him, and he responded, "*Émoi*," except she misunderstood and thought he said, "*Et moi*" ("And me"). Birkin teased him on the show, "And you and you and you, always." Gainsbourg reminded her they were supposed to be using just one word and said he had meant *émoi*, which means to be moved, or emote. When Birkin returned after filming to the home she shared with Doillon, she found a piece of paper stuck to the door. On it was written two words: *Et moi?* (And me?) It was signed: *Jacques*.

"Jacques (Doillon) is not a violent man at all," Birkin said in an interview in 1988. She was ostensibly promoting the Varda documentary but the conversation had turned to the men in her life. "I am frightened by the fact that violence does not scare me. Sometimes I wonder: Isn't what I'm looking for to prove my love? Loving unreasonably requires a kind of violence, or maybe it's me who is violent."

Her relationship with Doillon was already on shaky ground, and she felt like she had no room to deal with fixing it because two other important men in her life were suffering from rapidly declining health. By 1991, Birkin's father, David, had fallen ill. Around the same time, Gainsbourg started spending more time in and out of hospitals for cancer.

She was in London with her parents when she got a call on March 2, 1991, that Serge Gainsbourg had died from a heart attack at the age of sixty-two. He was supposed to travel to New Orleans the following Monday to record a jazz album. Just the night before, he had phoned to say he'd bought her a big diamond because she had lost one that he'd given her. She didn't take him seriously: "I said, 'Oh, stop drinking, Serge.'"

Gainsbourg died at home on the rue de Verneuil with Charlotte and Bambou by his side. Birkin talked to her mother all night while waiting for the first flight back to Paris in the morning. She went upstairs to say good night to her ailing father, but he had fallen asleep. She left early the next morning.

When she got back to Paris, just the sight of people going about their daily lives at the airport, picking up suitcases and hailing taxis, made her feel like she was in a haze. "My world was left in chaos, silence and darkness. Serge is dead. Impossible . . . everything seems fuzzy but with the precision of a nightmare," she wrote in her diary.

When she arrived at Gainsbourg's home, she was shocked to see crowds had already gathered en masse, singing "La Javanaise" and his other signature songs. For days following, the street would be shut down because of the fans' around-the-clock vigil.

Gainsbourg's valet let Birkin inside the house, where she found Charlotte, Kate, and Bambou cradling his dead body like the pietà. They weren't prepared to let him go. "We lay down beside him and time stopped," Charlotte Gainsbourg said. "People came to embalm him, so we could stay longer."

Finally, after a few days, Charlotte agreed to bury him in the cemetery in Montparnasse. Baudelaire, Man Ray, and Jean-Paul Sartre are also all buried there; it is the second-most-notable cemetery in Paris after Père-Lachaise in the 20th arrondissement. Gainsbourg shared the same plot where his mother and father were buried, with the names Olga and Joseph Ginsburg in script on one side and Gainsbourg on another. It was a prominent, visible spot worthy of a man who would not have wanted to be buried on a tucked-away path. Birkin left her beloved Munkey in the coffin with him.

After the burial, Birkin went with Bambou, Charlotte, and Kate to Birkin's place on rue de la Tour. The women crawled in bed together to silently mourn. They knew what was coming next would be observed by the world.

Gainsbourg's public funeral was mobbed as if for royalty. And for the French republic, maybe he was as close as it got. In attendance were groups of policemen and taxi drivers whom Gainsbourg had casually befriended throughout his life, often escorting him home when he was drunk. Catherine Deneuve and President François Mitterand read eulogies. The latter said of him: "He was our Baudelaire, our Apollinaire . . . he elevated the song to the level of art." Brigitte Bardot didn't come but sent a message: "I love him as a man but even more as a musician."

Before Birkin could even begin to process the emotional toll of Gainsbourg's early death, a second tragedy swallowed her up. The day before the public funeral for Gainsbourg, her father died. In the space of less than a week, Birkin had lost two of the most important men in her life—the only two, she wrote, who had loved her "unconditionally." She fell into a depression. "There are days when it's more muted, then like now: sharp and violent," she wrote in October 1991. She longed for Gainsbourg's physical presence, to be able to touch him or have a conversation. All she could feel was his absence—and her father's. "I wonder how to go on without Dad's advice. Without the exquisite smile, what's the point?" She let the depression envelop her.

Jacques Doillon, Jane Birkin's partner for a decade, felt their relationship could not keep up with her grief. By 1993, he had bought an apartment in the Latin Quarter as an office, saying that their place on rue de la Tour was too noisy. It was the same thing John Barry had done back in the late 1960s as their brief marriage was careening to an end. This move was under the guise of ease for his professional life; he was prolific as a director, sometimes shooting two films in one year. All of them, Birkin complained, seemed to be on location away from Paris. Their relationship was faltering, and now, with this second apartment, it was as if he had another life. She missed him and was jealous of the time he spent with actresses who had the youth and beauty that she believed was no longer her currency. She suspected that he was cheating, and she elliptically referred in her journals to someone confirming her suspicions. Finally, Doillon admitted it to her face: He had cheated. (He never confirmed this publicly.) She wrote that she felt like the floor had collapsed underneath her at that moment, but over time she admitted she was not surprised. In some ways Gainsbourg's death freed her up to deal with the reality that her decade-long relationship with Doillon had long been on ice. And with that final release, Birkin was able to gain the strength to ask Doillon to leave.

CHAPTER FIFTEEN

The Bag Is Going to Sing Now

To cope with her grief over the death of Serge Gainsbourg, Jane Birkin dove into her creative work with even more intensity, picking roles that were challenging, emotionally complex, and mature. After getting her start in the West End in London in the mid-'60s, it took Birkin almost twenty years to return to the stage, this time in French-language plays in Paris: *La fausse suivante* by Marivaux, directed by Patrice Chéreau in 1985; *L'ex-femme de ma vie* by Josiane Balasko in 1988; *Quelque part dans cette vie*, an adaptation of Israel Horovitz's *Park Your Car in Harvard Yard*, in 1990; Jean-Claude Carrière's *L'aide-mémoire* in 1993. She never felt totally at ease in plays even though she performed in them steadily through the '90s. She had stage fright and would feel heart palpitations and nausea. About twenty minutes into the play, she'd realized she was fine, but each performance brought a new threat of failure.

She auditioned for a 1995 production of Euripedes's *Women of Troy* at Britain's National Theatre. The play, which was originally produced in 415 BCE, is about the cost of war seen specifically through the eyes of women whose home, Troy, has been sacked, their husbands mostly killed. Birkin was trying out for Andromache, one of the group of Trojan women who were awaiting their fates, anticipating being shipped off to slavery and given away to Greek men. Director Annie Castledine's production was updated to contemporary times and set in a sports stadium, the kind where refugees are often sequestered.

Andromache was, crucially, a widow. When Birkin came in to meet with the director, Castledine did not let the persona of Jane Birkin influence her or who she presumed she was. In fact, she claimed not to have known who Birkin was prior to the audition. Instead, Castledine was moved by the sadness Birkin radiated, particularly when she spoke about her father and Gainsbourg dying in such close succession. The director told a journalist Birkin looked like her skin was barely holding on to her body. Castledine offered her the role, giving her twenty-four hours to think it over. Birkin didn't need that long; she accepted. She brought all the loss she had recently experienced in her life to the role: grief, anger, betrayal, abandonment. All in English, which was a language she rarely performed in. She got rave reviews in the production. "Those who know Jane Birkin solely through all that suborgasmic gasping on 'Je t'aime . . . moi non plus' can now get a crash career update on her at the National Theatre," wrote the *Independent*. Like Casteldine, critics noticed her haunting physical presence in particular, her body looking both fragile and in pain.

The three-month-long run of *Women of Troy* was a sweet homecoming to London. The longer she lived in France, the more she wondered if anyone remembered who she was in her native country. And, worse, she worried that if they did remember her, they found her a novelty, as if leaving home was all that was notable about her. Coming home to the theater and to England allowed Birkin to conquer two lingering sources of fear.

While she was in the Euripides production, an unnamed friend told her that Jacques Doillon had a new woman in his life. "My place was taken," Birkin wrote. "The one who said he could never love again, that he would never live with anyone again, that all he needed to be was alone." And yet her reaction was not deep melancholy but, rather, curiosity at his decision and the decisions of friends to try to dodge the truth about his dating life.

Birkin was redefining her life. In the mid-'90s, she was entering a time when she was content with being alone, or at least without a romantic partner for the first time since she was a teenager. She was on the verge of turning fifty and yet was experimenting with true independence for the first time. She kept herself remarkably busy, filming a role in the 1997 ensemble musical comedy *On connaît la chanson* (*Same Old Song*), directed by Alain Resnais, that was a smash hit in France, and also appeared in one of the less celebrated Merchant-Ivory films, 1998's *A Soldier's Daughter Never Cries*, as an eccentric single mother.

She also sold the home she had shared with Doillon on rue de la Tour and moved into a second-floor apartment on rue Jacob. Moving back to the Left Bank was a familiar comfort. She settled near Café de Flore and the gardens of the Église Saint-Germain-des-Prés, a few minutes on foot from her old house with Gainsbourg on rue de Verneuil. Birkin decorated the space with floral wallpaper and a jumble of flea market furniture, sofas covered in blankets, and photos and news clippings of her and her daughters, her bossy bulldog always following her around and either snoring or passing gas loudly. A journalist who visited said her decorating style reminded him of how an aristocratic student at Christ Church at the University of Oxford might have lived in the 1940s or '50s. Her family joked that she simply didn't care about order. "I'm incapable of throwing things away," she said, making a sly double entendre about material goods and, likely, the people in her life.

She toured again, sometimes presenting new compositions while consistently singing Serge Gainsbourg's. Birkin had never stopped performing Gainsbourg's songs for her. She thought of herself as his spokesperson, which seemed like a positive evolution for her grief. "People took it that I would never sing again because my composer was dead," Birkin wrote in her diary. It wasn't easy for her to sing the songs he had written for her, the ones from the height of their love, or the ones about the pain of the end of their relationship, but she felt singing them was her responsibility to his legacy—and theirs. "He wanted me to be the interpreter of those songs."

It was a topic that Birkin wrestled with constantly. In truth, she didn't even know if her ambition was to write her own songs. In her diary in 1998, she wondered if she even had the right to sing songs that weren't by Gainsbourg. A producer advised her it was because she had been so closely associated with one man, repeating a French idiom that roughly translates to "One is less unfaithful when there are several." Meanwhile, her daughter Charlotte was not interested in being "the guardian of the Gainsbourg-Birkin temple," according to one interviewer who asked her. "My mother has continued my father's work after his death and has been paying tribute to him for 30 years."

Birkin was famous enough that she was able to make a career touring and playing grand concert venues such as Carnegie Hall, but her relevance had waned despite efforts to the contrary. She was presented almost as a nostalgia act. She recorded new interpretations of her songs with Gainsbourg using North African musicians on her 2002 album *Arabesque*, which she toured around the world. In 2004, a *Guardian* critic wrote, "When Jane Birkin floats on to the stage wearing a red dress, there's an audible intake of breath. When she begins to dance, cheers ring out. In truth, it's not a very good dance, not in the traditional sense anyway. There's a gypsy [*sic*] abandon to it mixed with the leaps of a desert shaman, the sway of a sex kitten, the gangliness of a teenager . . ." They also pointed out that her audience could not get enough of it. She was a grown-up woman-child singing songs written for her by a dead lover.

Birkin was not the type to ever speak publicly about money, but touring was her only reliable income—taking smaller parts in European films was not going to make her a huge salary. Nor did she sign for a major book deal or an ad campaign that might have allowed her to cash in on her name or life experience. She was a star with an ego underneath her humble trappings. She loved the adulation from the crowd and she loved celebrating Gainsbourg's heyday, of which she had been an instrumental part. Maybe she was trying to right what she considered her own mother's wrong turn of leaving the stage and rarely returning.

She did not triumph in her music with the critical establishment, which consistently compared her to her younger self. "If she finds herself—perhaps with increasing irritation—still occupying the 'tragic muse' slot, it is because so much of what she says only underlines the divide—alternately mourning the death of both Serge and her father," wrote a review in the *New Statesman*. The London *Evening Standard* called her "sort of delightful, but I couldn't really begin to explain to you exactly where the talent lies. The voice is okay, but you have to know which bell to ring to find it. Jane Birkin is not quite enough of a chanteuse to get away with rolling up on stage and telling us which end of love is squishy."

They weren't wrong. Her musical persona had not moved on from the hits of the 1960s and '70s, unlike her output as an actor onscreen and onstage, where she had demonstrated a much more nuanced sensibility. *Le Monde* called her "a servant of the past" and noted that, as a singer, "she benefited from the public's sympathy." According to the *Evening Standard*'s critic, "In an ideal world she might be getting together with Phil Spector, who may have some time on his hands"—he was in the midst of being prosecuted for murder—"or Phil Collins, because we don't know exactly what he's up to at the moment. Or Sting. Or Bono." What Birkin needed, these reviews all seemed to say, was another Svengali who was inspired by her, someone whose work she could interpret with her signature charm. As if she could never be a creative being on her own or without a powerful man by her side.

Small humiliations never ended. She was often faced with the dilemma of leaving a storied concert hall through the stage door, feeling content after having performed a good show, and being approached by someone with a photo to sign—and it would be a nude shot from thirty or forty years earlier. Having been raised to be polite, she'd quickly scrawl her signature on the bottom, but she found the whole charade depressing. Or people would ask if she was the same Birkin as the bag. She'd say, "Yes, and the bag is going to sing now!"

Birkin prided herself on staying not just open-minded, but politically progressive. Many fellow French stars of her era grew conservative, including Alain Delon, her costar from *La piscine*, who supported the far-right National Front party; Brigitte Bardot, who was anti-immigration and has been fined more than once for her public statements; and Gérard Depardieu, who was found guilty of sexually assaulting two women (which he has denied and his lawyers stated they would appeal) and favored spending time with dictators and despots. Given Serge Gainsbourg's love of money and guns and the French police and hatred of taxes, it seems plausible that, had he lived, he would have been leaning further and further right as the years went on. But Birkin's devotion to left-leaning humanitarian work seemed, if anything, to grow stronger as she aged.

Her political life started young, at just twelve years old, when she marched in the streets of London alongside her father against capital punishment. In the 1970s in France, she campaigned for four women on trial for helping a high school student who had been sexually assaulted get an abortion. In 2007, she told a radio show host that she would always fight for immigrants coming to France because she was one too: "I was welcomed perhaps because I was pretty and English, and it is infinitely easier than if I came from North Africa."

Over her lifetime, Birkin made humanitarian trips to Tibet, Rwanda, and Burma (now Myanmar) and worked with Amnesty International concerning the AIDS crisis and immigrant welfare. In the spring of 2002, Birkin, Kate Barry, Lou Doillon, and Charlotte Gainsbourg all marched together against the far-right candidate Jean-Marie Le Pen. Birkin's bag even became a political prop, covered prominently with the flag of Tibet, which seemed to have been stuck onto the leather with packing tape.

On occasion her sentiments sounded out of touch with the people she was trying to help. "I asked my mother, 'What did you take when your apartment was bombed in the Second World War?'—and she answered 'Schiaparelli Shocking perfume. When you're losing everything, it's what makes you feel good that counts,'" Birkin recounted. She took that advice quite literally and walked down the rue de Passy—a street lined with jewelers, high-end grocers, and the kinds of stores that sell monogrammed cashmere socks—shopping for refugees, for whom she bought Guerlain lipstick and silk underwear. A luxurious item can certainly give anyone a momentary lift in spirits. Birkin's approach would have been more condemnable if she hadn't also been so dedicated to hands-on volunteer work.

Activism was always part of her platform, but as she aged, she talked about it more openly. On the whole, Birkin was someone who was culturally informed and well-read and interested in the world around her. Her access to people in power was something she did not hesitate to leverage. In 2008, President Nicolas Sarkozy granted her an audience to talk about the morality of France's oil dealings with Myanmar. A longtime supporter of Sein Win, head of Myanmar's self-proclaimed government-in-exile, and then opposition leader Aung San Suu Kyi, Birkin was an outspoken critic of the French energy company Total and its ties to the Burmese military junta, and advocated for divestment. But her activism could sometimes come off as self-serving. Some of it involved talking about issues she cared about onstage, but it's hard to know if anyone who came to see her sing "Je t'aime . . . moi non plus" cared to hear it.

On one of her activist sojourns in the summer of 1995, fresh off her run as Andromache in *Women of Troy*, Birkin headed to Sarajevo, working with the André Malraux Cultural Centre to take books to people living there under siege. While there in August, she met the writer Olivier Rolin, and they got to know each other, sometimes traveling by tank together while smoking cigarettes. She sent her mother a fax from the trip saying that she'd met a man, that he was a writer, he had been one of the activists in May '68. They had in fact come across each other in Paris over the years but had never properly been introduced. She'd had a passing interest in Rolin, even a bit of a crush on, this "rather chic man with intellectual glasses and polished shoes." He was creative, like John Barry and Serge Gainsbourg and Jacques Doillon, but he wasn't volatile. In that sense, he was different from her usual type. She nicknamed him Tiger. "I have never seen such an honest guy," she wrote. "He is funny in life, righteously angry and impertinent, loyal and disarming." She couldn't believe it, but she thought she loved him. She wondered if maybe he would be her last love.

His impression of her was that she was lonely and unhappy when they met.

But despite his even temper, she was still capable of getting in a fight and making a scene as she had with all her other partners. At a dinner party in Paris, she once threw a glass of wine in his face—he could not remember the cause of the argument—and said she only wished she had the whole bottle. "She was irresistible, even in anger," he said.

He was smitten with her. He wrote, "Jane walking on the beach, her linen shirt blowing in the wind, a pencil in her hair, simplicity and bareness. Jane at home in Paris, under the dark printed fabrics, the hangings, the frills, the garlands, the chandeliers, the stuffed animals, the photos, the knick-knacks of memory: an eccentric Englishwoman." Invigorated by her new love, he moved in with her on rue Jacob on the Left Bank in 1996. Birkin felt optimistic too. She wanted a baby with him, even though she was nearly fifty and already a grandmother when they met. But it never got that far—he didn't want another child. She considered marrying him, writing in her journal wistfully that she always thought of marriage when she saw old people walking arm in arm on the street, but thought it was too late.

But not everyone was happy. Her daughter Lou, by then thirteen years old, told her she was worried that Rolin would take the place of her father, though Birkin denied that anyone could ever replace Doillon. Olivier Rolin was a true partner, and finding love, at any age, is a beautiful thing. But Lou was picking up on something her mother didn't sense, which was that, for all the independence she wanted, she was a serial monogamist who was falling into old habits. Or a more generous view was that Birkin was allowing herself to indulge in her own desires. Birkin might have been centering her life on men and love once again, but at this age, it was in addition to, not instead of, a fully realized life and career.

CHAPTER SIXTEEN

Autofiction

Jane Birkin, wrote, directed, and starred in one film: *Boxes*. It was her life's work in two senses. The film was her singular vision, and it was also transparently about her own personal history. The project was the work of nearly two decades. She began working on the screenplay in 1992 to process the grief about her father's death but she didn't make the movie until 2006, when she was almost sixty years old. *Boxes* follows the life of a middle-aged woman, Anna (played by Birkin). Birkin wanted to direct and write the film but she didn't intend to act in it. In fact, she handpicked the actress Rosanna Arquette to play Anna, but she was already committed to a TV movie. Birkin ended up taking the part herself. It was a way for her to dig into her role as full auteur, controlling each key element of the film.

Anna lives in her French country home and has three daughters with whom she has warm and playful relationships: Fanny, the eldest (Natacha Régnier, loosely representing Kate Barry); Camille (Lou Doillon, playing a Charlotte Gainsbourg stand-in); and Lilly (Adèle Exarchopoulos, who is the Lou Doillon character). And then there are her three exes, each one, as in real life, a father to one of her three daughters: an unnamed English novelist (John Hurt) who was largely unsupportive; Max, the creative genius who didn't wear socks (Maurice Bénichou), whom Anna seems by far the most fond of; and Jean, the unfaithful ex (Tchéky Karyo), who is the only one still alive yet held in much lower regard than the dead.

The casting of the movie adds to the feeling of it being a family affair. Besides casting Lou as one of her daughters, for the father role Birkin chose her frequent costar Michel Piccoli, who had played her father in Jacques Doillon's *The Prodigal Daughter* and her husband in *La belle noiseuse*. Birkin's own mother was supposed to play Anna's mother, but Judy Campbell's health was declining over the years Birkin worked on the script, and she was in and out of the hospital, first for a broken hip, then pneumonia and bronchial issues. In her late eighties and hospitalized, Campbell was so dedicated to working on her daughter's movie that she was trying to learn her lines from her hospital bed. About a month before filming was set to start, the family decided she was too ill to take on filming, so Birkin's friend of many years, Geraldine Chaplin (Charlie Chaplin's daughter), took the part of her mother, even though she was born in 1944, just two years before Birkin.

Boxes' plot is centered on Anna's country house in Brittany, which is nearly overtaken by moving boxes that need to be dealt with. The act of unpacking them with her family milling about opens up memories of all the lives that she has lived. She spends the film meeting and reckoning with the most important figures in her life: parents, lovers, children. The title *Boxes* could be interpreted literally: the boxes Anna unpacks. Or as a symbol for Pandora's box, each one she opens taking her through a different scenario in her life to process.

In one long scene, Camille, the middle daughter played by Lou, wanders in and thinks one of the notes to her mom wishing her a good night was written by her. She finds another saved note written to Anna's last partner, Jean, pledging her love for him. "It's strange for a mother to have a daughter. You want her to like her stepfather. You do everything for it to work out. It's awful when it doesn't work," Anna says to Camille. "Then it works too well. You get a strange feeling. Your heart pounds when you see them walking off, hand in hand. All of a sudden you feel excluded." The dialogue, which is delivered quietly and matter-of-factly, could be read as Anna feeling left out when Camille and Jean forge their own bond. Or it could, as with so many of Birkin's projects touching on taboos and sexuality, be interpreted as having more overtly incestuous undertones. Camille cries when she reflects on that time in her life, saying she felt sidelined by the new relationship.

The film resists over-the-top drama. There is plenty of crying and even some shouting between characters, but the emotions in each conversation change rapidly. Just moments after talking about Jean, Anna and Camille start joking about Camille's feet and the two other daughters come in with a roast chicken they all pick at. Camille unearths another notebook with a note written to Anna and Max, her own father, then casually points out that Max, who is long dead, is standing outside under a tree, waiting to speak to Anna. The plot rolls along like this, mixing hard truths with moments of levity and magical realism.

Olivier Rolin, to whom Birkin remained romantically attached until 2008, compared it to Ulysses encountering his distraught mother in the kingdom of shadows in *The Odyssey*. In the preface to the 2021 published script of *Boxes*, Rolin offered another interpretation of the title: "We could also read this word in a pugilistic sense, because it is a fight that the characters are engaged in."

Boxes was filmed over six weeks in 2006 at Birkin's own house in the Finistère region of Brittany. As much of a Parisian as she had become, she spent a lot of time being slow in the countryside, reading papers, drinking tea, one of her series of bulldogs napping on a threadbare sofa. The house was lived in, but in an enchanting way. Exarchopoulos, who played the youngest daughter and who has gone on to become one of the most celebrated young actors in France, told a magazine that she remembered going into one of Birkin's own bathrooms to wash her hands and seeing a claw-foot bathtub for the first time in her life. Next to it was a bowl of miniature Toblerones. She told Birkin how cool she thought that was, and Birkin invited her to stay over for the night and eat chocolates in a bath anytime she wanted.

Boxes is a film whose plot is so porous, so literally taken from Birkin's personal life, that the term "*roman à clef*" does not do it justice. The better word for this genre is "autofiction," the same in French and English—a story so thinly veiled, there are no guessing games to play about who or what the material is based on. It gives the viewer the satisfaction of guessing who the characters represent but without much effort. Anna's style is nearly identical to how Birkin dressed in middle age; she spends the film wearing an oversize men's striped shirt, chinos rolled at the ankles, and an old brown silk tie as a belt.

Like Birkin, the Anna character is a warm but inquisitive, even needy mother. Throughout the film, she wants to know what her daughters really think of her as a parent. Guilt hovers over her words when she tells them, "You were delivered without instructions, you had to figure it out!" *Boxes* examines the mother-daughter dynamic with a critical eye toward herself. In the film, she says, "I did everything wrong. I got everything wrong. I hurt children. I only remember what I want to remember. Perhaps it was all my fault."

Each of the exes, on the other hand, gets a searing scene of reappraisal. To know anything about Jane Birkin was to know the rough outlines of her romantic history. First Anna sees Max, the Serge Gainsbourg character, who tells her that their story was impeccable, Shakespearean, immortal. Later she enters a dusty room, and her ex Jean, who most resembled Jacques Doillon, is inside. Their discussion immediately turns heated, with them lying on the floor together. Anna wonders what it was like for him to have sex with other women during their seven years together. "Is this how it was? On the floor?" she said. "To think I left Max for you. You are and always have been ordinary." Jean intones dramatically that Max was inescapable, that his portrait was on every wall. He slaps her and says, "There was no room for me. His death pulled us apart."

She finally works out her feelings about her brief marriage to John Barry: "I was seventeen, and I loved you," she says to the Barry character. Then she lapses into a free association, channeling her teenage self speaking: "A baby would prove that I love you. I'm not much of a lover, but I can learn." He is shown as such an absentee father that his own daughter barely knows him, and Anna hardly remembers what brought them together in the first place. The animosity goes both ways. "Your memory, Anna, is as selective as a washing machine," he says.

Jean comes away from the film looking the worst, which is perhaps because when she was beginning to work on the script in the '90s, her long relationship with Doillon had recently ended. Birkin wrote in her diaries about her jealousy of the actresses he worked with and the eventual cheating that brought about the end of their liaison, but she spoke about him far less than her other exes. Nor did she ever recount physical abuse. Either Doillon's character is the most fictionalized or through *Boxes* she finally shares the real dynamic between them. If Birkin was working out her grief over her father and Gainsbourg, whose *Boxes* stand-ins come across as caring if flawed men who genuinely loved Anna, she was working out her rage against Doillon. Birkin and Doillon's time together had been portrayed as more placid than her previous ones, so the animosity was news, at least to the casual viewer.

Birkin thought *Boxes* was about family, and most of all about mothers and daughters. She did not see it as centered on men. That, too, is how Birkin saw her own life. Her public portrayal as muse and halves of various power-couple relationships was not constructed by her. They were vital episodes of her history, but they were not how she defined herself. Men were important chapters in her life, but they were far from the whole story.

Boxes was acclaimed and selected for the 2007 Cannes Film Festival's Un Certain Regard program, which focuses on less traditional films that deserve recognition. The paper *Le Figaro* noted its "worrying, unpredictable, and touching sincerity." Like much of Birkin's work in French, the film had a negligible presence in the United States and the United Kingdom save for hard-core fans of Birkin or foreign cinephiles.

Boxes is not necessarily Birkin's greatest work of acting; or rather, it's not a showy one. Anna is the least theatrical character in the movie. But it is still her most important artistic creation. She did not seek to make a biopic of herself with *Boxes*, but a tender tone poem on aging, and in the process it served as an appraisal of her life and the choices she had made.

The film is a statement of self, another format for Birkin as artist to reflect on her life and show the world how she saw herself from the inside rather than how her life had been portrayed from the outside. In one scene at the very end there is even a nod to the afterlife, although Birkin had maintained all her life that she was not religious at all, but rather an admirer of humanity. Anna meets one final person at the very end: a young girl, maybe six years old, looking out the window. Anna takes her hand and leads her downstairs. "What's your name?" Anna asks. The girl looks at her and answers, "Anna." It's herself as a child. It is a scene that comes off a bit maudlin—the inner child is a little too obvious—but also feels significant in the context of this magnum opus on selfhood. Birkin has come full circle in reckoning with her parents, lovers, and daughters, and is ready to focus back on her own self as she ages.

CHAPTER SEVENTEEN

And You're as Pretty as Ever

When *Boxes* came out in 2007, Birkin told *Vogue*, "I'm not saying I'm eternally a girl, but I think I got old in a Patti Smith sort of stringy way." Birkin thought all women looked best around forty. "It's the sort of age where I find that there's a blossoming. It's what they've left behind, it's what's coming up, it's the fragility of adolescence into middle age," she said in 2020, when she was in her early seventies. Forty was when she made her live singing debut at Bataclan, wearing an agnès b. men's shirt and big pants. She thought her way of dressing was a perfectly comfortable uniform for a woman in middle age and beyond, even chic. But not everyone agreed. Michael Coste, her sales associate at Hermès where she'd buy her own yearly planners or a gift, always urged her to at least try on a coat or a dress from the women's section in this era. She would roll her eyes; she didn't want to dress like a woman any longer. She wasn't sure she even cared that much about fashion. She liked the contrast of bold menswear against the fragility of an aging woman. "When I see photos of me from 1968, my big doll eyes underlined with eyeliner, exaggerated mouth, bangs, I find it horrible. . . . It's like makeup, at a certain age—stop playing with false eyelashes. Otherwise, it becomes terrifying," she said.

Coco Chanel supposedly said, "Once you reach a certain stage in life, you have the face that you deserve." As she aged, Birkin decided to forgo cosmetic procedures in favor of the face of a woman who smoked, tanned, and enjoyed life, except for an occasional injection of something in the Botox family for her forehead wrinkles. (She didn't like the look of a frown.) Her resistance was a very specific, almost anti-capitalist way of rebelling against gender norms. She used to say publicly that the best facelift was smiling. Privately she would ask friends if she should get her eyes done or treat sagging in the lower half of her face. "I have flat lips like Dad's," she told her daughter Charlotte. "A doctor told me yesterday, 'Your lips will completely disappear unless you do something about it.'" She always kept a sense of humor, but she wielded it to evade her real feelings and inner conflict about aging in public.

Jane Birkin was with her daughter Lou Doillon at a bus stop when someone came up to Lou, a singer and songwriter, and said, "Oh God, I just love what you write." "And then they looked at me and said, 'And you're as pretty as ever,' and I thought, 'Oh, I wish they had complimented me on my work.'" That old dichotomy of being pretty or being smart was particularly unfair to women like Birkin, who were both.

The specter of how mothers pass on their feelings about their beauty and aging—their inheritance—was something Birkin discussed in interviews. "One day my mother said to me, 'I saw myself in the mirror and I said to myself, it's gone, it's over.' But what's gone? I asked her. 'Well, my beauty!' It irritated me, I thought: my God, what pride to want to be beautiful when you are an old lady," she said. "And then, one day, it happened to me, I didn't recognize myself in the mirror. I understand Mom in almost everything today, I feel like I've become her." She went even further in another anecdote: "I recently said to my daughter Lou Doillon, 'It's gone.' And she's like, 'What's gone, Mum?' And I said, 'My beauty.' It's like you wake up one day and suddenly the outside doesn't correspond to the inside anymore. I've adjusted my thinking a bit since then. The essential thing, I now think, is a good sense of humor. Thankfully, my girls have that too."

Birkin knew she had wrinkles and age spots, and that she didn't have the body of a twenty-one-year-old anymore. She wasn't going to get cosmetic surgery to try to change it, but living with her corporeal body was not an easy détente. Her relationship with her own body and face as she aged corresponded to both her high expectations of herself and her need to please others. She was afraid of disappointing people with her own physical appearance, which she described as stout and portly. The language she used about it was beyond self-deprecating; she was harsh. "I try to tell myself I don't mind for there are so many women I love whose faces look like elephants' knees. I thought I'd get used to having wrinkles all over," she said. Feeling pretty is a difficult thing to preserve; being professionally pretty is even harder to maintain.

When Birkin was in her mid-seventies, Charlotte Gainsbourg asked her at what point she would stop—or had stopped—caring about her looks. Birkin's answer to her middle child was that she thought she personally had already reached that point. She wanted to remove mirrors from her home, stop thinking about what she looked like, and do other things. To be in the world, unfettered by expectation.

Birkin came from fairly healthy stock. Her father was in his late seventies when he died in 1991; her mother died in 2004 at the age of eighty-eight, dressed in the hospital in pearls and silk pajamas and insisting everyone in the family gather to drink champagne together before she passed. Birkin smoked—at one point chain-smoking three packs per day—like so many people of her generation, but her nights of downing cocktails until dawn had mostly ended along with her relationship to Serge Gainsbourg. Her daughter Lou described her as the kind of parent who was constantly on the go and preoccupied with the needs of others. "She made me food, then food for the theater crew, brought three chickens to the local homeless, took care of her dying father, picked up her mother at the hospital, jumped on a plane," she said. Birkin's main issue was with insomnia, and taking sleeping pills—usually a benzodiazepine called Lexomil—nightly. She complained that her doctors never gave her enough to really knock her out. At parties she would take one at the end of the night and would offer them around to guests. But, for the most part, she was healthy.

In 1998, Birkin was diagnosed with leukemia, which she dismissed as an "easy" cancer, always one to play down her own pain. The treatment was successful, but it brought on another form of leukemia that required radiotherapy and chemotherapy. She was not an easy patient in that she was headstrong and didn't prioritize her health over her work life or her social life. She went on a vacation to Türkiye with Garbielle Crawford right after doing multiple chemotherapy sessions because she didn't want to change her plans—or acknowledge how sick she really was. Birkin would end up checking into the hospital when she was depleted and could no longer stand the pain. By then she considered the hospital her second home; at one point she was undergoing three blood transfusions a week. But she would get treatments, taking a taxi to the American Hospital of Paris in Neuilly in the western suburbs, then get another taxi home, feed her dogs, and go out for dinner or to a play or perform her own concerts. Her children saw how worn-out she was and chose to blame her professional team for forcing her to appear onstage. But it was Birkin's idea. She didn't want being ill to define how she lived her life.

Birkin became a grandmother many times over, including to Kate Barry's son Roman de Kermadec; Charlotte Gainsbourg's children Ben, Alice, and Jo Attal; and Lou Doillon's sons Marlowe Mitchell and Laszlo Keats Miller Manel, who are twenty years apart in age. All three of her daughters had children fairly young, just like their mother did: Barry and Doillon were each almost twenty, and Gainsbourg was in her mid-twenties. "One of the reasons I felt that I could take responsibility for having a child when I was nineteen was that my mother was very strong and showed me the way," said Doillon. "With such a complicated profession where women often sacrifice their personal life, she gave me the opportunity to do her job, to be taken seriously and, at the same time, to embark on family and children. Total freedom, and a freedom that does not care about the judgments of others."

Birkin's three girls also all went into creative pursuits: photography for Kate, acting for Gainsbourg, and modeling and music for Doillon. In 2005, Barry had a photo exposition on the Left Bank, near Serge Gainsbourg's house on rue de Verneuil. Birkin was so touched, she cried upon viewing the show. The family all stuck around, moving on to a restaurant after the opening where they stayed until 1 a.m. Kate ate steak frites and seemed less fragile than usual. Birkin was glad her daughter was making a name for herself on her own. "At first, I was better known because of my family: my mother, my stepfather, my father, my sisters. . . . Now I hope I'm known a bit more for my own work," Barry said.

Kate was truly talented, and shot for pretty much every women's and fashion magazine: *Elle*, *Vogue*, *Vanity Fair*, *Marie Claire*, *Harper's Bazaar*, *Paris Match*. *Cosmopolitan* magazine asked her in 2000 to submit a self-portrait. For it, she wore a pair of jeans upside down. The jeans were pulled over her long arms raised above her head, the back of her head was where the butt would be, and her nose, mouth, and chin stuck out of the fly in profile, with a lit cigarette dangling from her lips. The image is both surreal and stylized. It was a favorite of Birkin's. Sylvain Besson, a photography curator, described Kate's work as her way of navigating her own space and showing her personality: "Initially surrounded by the images of others before becoming a producer of icons herself."

Charlotte Gainsbourg became the most famous of Birkin's children, particularly outside of France, breaking through in international cinema with directors like the Mexican filmmaker Alejandro González Iñárritu and Danish filmmaker Lars von Trier. Her angular face and intensely reserved demeanor gave her an air of melancholy that was made for the screen. Her work with von Trier in particular was provocative, with a lot of graphic depictions of sex and violence. One could point to her father as the source of her talent, but her raw but muted presence onscreen came from her mother. Charlotte starred in von Trier's so-called Depression trilogy of movies: *Antichrist*, *Melancholia*, and *Nymphomaniac*, a five-hour-long film about a sex addict. She was proud to be his muse. Gainsbourg would call her mother with talk of the next day's script, shocked but amused about the contents. They shared a dark sense of humor, cackling together at whatever prosthetics Gainsbourg would have to wear or which shocking behavior she was about to commit to film.

Lou Doillon was the baby of the family, more than a decade younger than her sisters. She sometimes felt invisible as a child against the emotional swirl of the rest of the family. Birkin was nostalgic, and her father Jacques Doillon was melancholic; Lou, meanwhile, was a born observer. "I spent my time under the tables and I was sensitive to the contradiction between the eloquent speeches and the nervous gestures of the hands and feet observed under the table." Lou was also the daughter who was the most outwardly critical of the way she was raised and her family unit, in a manner that was candid yet gentle. "It's important to understand that I come from a family that lives in the cult of Peter Pan. We all live the lives of children," she said.

Lou also had a rebellious streak. She started ditching school regularly at fourteen to smoke pot with her friends. So Birkin was relieved when, at fifteen, Lou was offered a role in a film. As Birkin recalled, it entailed the character giving blow jobs to the boys at school. "She got the part and I said, 'Go for it.' She had no naked scenes or anything like that; it was just a very impertinent part. And she got it." That was Birkin's parenting style: free from moralizing and heavy on support of any creative pursuits. Lou could be a wildchild but acting settled her down. She turned out to be the biggest polymath of all of them, modeling for Miu Miu, making music, and exhibiting her own drawings.

All of Birkin's daughters were, loosely put, creative types who dabbled across disciplines. They never suffered from the discourse around nepotism, and as a proud and doting mother and the daughter of an actress in her own right, Birkin didn't question the legitimacy of their careers in the arts. Following in the footsteps of one's parents may have seemed not just normal but inevitable.

What is much more notable is the mythmaking around Jane Birkin's daughters. They became the embodiment of Parisian chic in a different way than their mother had. Birkin was an English girl who charmed France with her personal style. Her daughters were born with a pedigree, and their personae as perfect *Parisiennes* were tied to a kind of innate cool. They were visible to the public from birth. They were also naturally gamine, a French term meaning attractively boyish, and they all modeled or worked around fashion.

Barry contributed to the creation of the French woman, albeit behind the camera. Besides the many famous French women she took portraits of for magazines, she shot a campaign for the French contemporary brand Comptoir des Cotonniers called *Mère et Fille* in which chic mothers and their daughters both dressed in the brand. One can consider it the Parisian woman myth fulfilled. The duos are of the type where the mother and daughter look almost the same age; where the mom wears boots and a jacket with a diagonal zipper and looks as cool as the daughter. The message was loud and clear: that a family helps create a legacy of style.

"Neither daughter feels she has her mother's beauty, and objectively, if you compare them with footage of the peachy, dewy twenty-two-year-old Birkin, it's true," wrote American *Vogue* in a 2009 profile of Gainsbourg and Doillon titled "Skinny Genes." In it, Charlotte sips a soup, and Doillon has nothing at lunchtime. Of their bodies, Doillon said, "We don't starve ourselves or anything. That's what's kind of sickening. Our eldest sister is even skinnier than either of us, and she's eating all the time. Family rumor is that there is so much tuberculosis from generation to generation that maybe there's something in the blood that would explain that weird thing that we are *all* like this. You look at my uncle, aunt, even grandmother—she was very tall and thin, everything very, very angular and small." They helped carve out a French female aesthetic of women who were thin and effortlessly chic from adolescence through their old age.

For all of Birkin's self-effacement about entering her menopausal years and aging disgracefully, she remained prominent within the world of fashion. In 2000, she walked the runway for the Belgian designer Martin Margiela's highly coveted ready-to-wear clothing collections for Hermès, as did Charlotte. The fine knits and loose, slightly masculine trousers suited her own personal style. Birkin looked comfortable; she looked herself. She modeled for Hedi Slimane when he was at Dior and Celine, but not in gowns or frilly blouses or lacquered with makeup. Instead she wore dark suits and tuxedos. She collaborated with brands such as A.P.C., for which, in 2022, she designed a capsule version of her own daily wardrobe: T-shirts and jeans, workman-style trousers with pockets for keys and a wallet on errands, some sweaters, a coat, sneakers, a straw bag.

In 2006, she worked with the perfume house Miller Harris on a fragrance called L'Air de Rien, literally the "feeling of nothing," or more accurately, "nonchalantly." "I wanted it to smell like my brother's hair, my father's pipe, dusty old books, the Metro in the old days," she said. It's a musk with notes of patchouli, neroli, vanilla, and oak moss that smells airy, powdery, and vaguely funky, almost like lived-in upholstery. She didn't tell her daughters she was working on a perfume, but after it came out, they started spotting it; Charlotte saw it in the Parisian department store Le Bon Marché, and Lou found it in New York. Unlike the Birkin bag, it did not and was not meant to capture the imagination of the masses. Smelling like Grandmother's curtains on a rainy Sunday morning is not for everyone, but those who love it find it haunting and delicious. But that was how Birkin was choosing to age. Rather than defying the aging process or ignoring her own preferences in favor of what might be more crowd-pleasing, she dug in. If Jane Birkin was going to age in the public eye, it was going to be on her own terms.

CHAPTER EIGHTEEN
Afraid of Solitude

Jane Birkin was worried about her eldest daughter, Kate Barry. Her father, John Barry, died of a heart attack in February 2011 at seventy-seven years old in New York, where he had lived for the past few decades. Kate, who was forty-four at the time, was in the Philippines. Though his involvement in her life had been less than reliable, Birkin wanted to be supportive of whatever emotions Kate was going through. She offered to fly out and assist her daughter, but Kate asked her to stay home in Paris and take care of her son, Roman. Birkin hoped being of service to Kate would help her navigate what would be an emotionally trying time for anyone, let alone her daughter, who had been dealing with substance abuse since the 1980s.

If Birkin was still trying to come to terms with her relationship with the only man she had ever married, she did it in a quiet way. She conducted a few interviews about him for the press but was otherwise reserved about his passing. On the Sunday after his death, she walked a few minutes from her home on rue Jacob down to Église Saint-Germain to light some candles. She cried for him and then went home and consulted two "shrinks"—her term—to get her head in order.

Birkin was instead mostly focused on how Kate would cope. Kate Barry's addiction issues did not end in her teens, and she had gone to a series of rehabilitation treatment centers over the years. One such stint, at the Broadway Lodge, ended up being such a success that she decided she wanted to help create similar places in France—but, unlike the private clinics, these centers would be true to the socialized medicine of France, where no one would have to pay out of pocket for treatment. It took years, but in 1994 Barry did manage to open a center two hours from Paris called La Maison de Kate, with help from Georgina Dufoix, the minister of health. The rehab was in a castle in Bucy-le-Long in Aisne that had previously welcomed vagrants, and helped addicts recover via talk therapy, which was what Kate had found the most helpful for her own sobriety. Birkin saw how excited Kate was to see the first clients coming in and how seriously she took that responsibility. Birkin liked to tell how, every so often, she would be out in public and find a note someone had left her thanking Kate for saving someone's life.

The unfortunate truth is that a lifelong battle with drugs and alcohol, especially one that starts during adolescence, is not going to be a simple linear narrative of addiction and rehabilitation. Kate's son Roman said, "She started drinking a little again, from time to time. I could see that she wasn't handling it well." But she also appeared happy. In January 2013, Kate was seeing the film producer Oury Milshtein, who professed he wanted to marry her, which Birkin wholeheartedly approved of. But they were on and off as a couple and would continue to be.

During an evening in October 2013, Birkin noted in her diary, her whole family was together for dinner. Barry was joyous, in great form. But that increasingly felt like an anomaly.

Just a few weeks later, in November, Birkin noticed that Kate's face looked swollen, which she assumed was from tears. Gabrielle Crawford also thought she had been looking a bit unhappy and fragile, but she and Kate had been planning a birthday party for Birkin, some kind of outdoor tented affair in the garden. They sent out invitations and ordered Middle Eastern food and a cake shaped like an enormous Birkin bag.

The last time her mother saw her, Barry talked about her rampant fears: She was afraid of solitude; she was afraid of not having enough money as she was preparing to move to an apartment on rue

Claude-Chahu, near the place on rue de la Tour where Birkin and Jacques Doillon had lived for many years. "I hugged her dearly," she wrote. Birkin thought Kate was just stressed-out and overly anxious, that she simply needed some comfort and a good night's sleep.

Just a few weeks later, on December 11, 2013, Kate Barry died at age forty-six, just three days before her mother's sixty-seventh birthday.

The details around her death were sparse. What is known is that her body was found around 6:30 p.m. on the pavement outside her building.

Birkin was essentially frozen with emotional pain. She had to go to the police station along with Charlotte, Kate's son Roman, her boyfriend Milshtein, and Gabrielle Crawford. They were placed in separate rooms and questioned about the accident. There was no one else in the apartment, and the door was locked from the inside. Police found antidepressants, which Roman, then twenty-five, confirmed his mother was taking for depression. Suicide was suspected but never proven. When they were all allowed to return home, Crawford and Birkin crawled onto the bed together holding hands, draped in silence.

They kept the planned birthday party for Birkin but turned it into a small, somber memorial for friends and family, complete with the Birkin bag cake. Barry's funeral was held a week after she died, at Église Saint-Roch in Paris. It was attended by her large extended family and celebrities like Catherine Deneuve, Isabelle Huppert, Carla Bruni, and Charlotte Rampling. Throughout the service, songs written by John Barry were played, including themes to *The Lion in Winter* and *Midnight Cowboy*. In the middle of it all, next to the altar, was the self-portrait Kate had taken in jeans and with a cigarette between her lips. Cool and nonchalant to the end.

The death came at a precarious time for Birkin. The devastation she experienced could not be understated. For the next six months she barely ate anything and would stay up until the early hours of morning, then sleep in until 2 or 3 p.m. And her own health had been declining as the leukemia had come back around 2010. In

2012, she was hospitalized for lung issues, and was treated with chemotherapy that same year. She didn't want to tell her daughters it had come back, but they could tell—she was starting to look ill. Birkin tried to be self-deprecating about it. Years into battling cancer, she complained jokingly that the treatments "made me hideously fat. If I'd realized how monstrous I looked waddling around, I wouldn't have gone out."

The depth of her devastation can be marked by the fact that she stopped writing in her journal on December 11, 2013, after more than fifty years of recording her life. She was incapable of continuing after Kate's death; she lost her confidence in herself and as a mother. "How could I write after that? . . . It was like I was living a parallel life. The carpet had been pulled from under my feet. I fell ill . . . and why not," she wrote as an addendum to her last entry in *Post-Scriptum*, the second installment of her diaries. She wondered if she had only acted differently: calling Kate more frequently, or forcing her to come on tour with her in order to keep a closer eye on her. "You invent different versions. Even if it won't change anything. That's how it is. And you can go back in time for years doing this, wondering if things would have happened differently if only you had done something better."

She had good days when she took her friends and her dogs out to restaurants and paid for everyone. But her bad days were frequent: She felt ugly, depressed, and jealous of the careers of her contemporaries. She lost her optimism. The curtain, she said, was drawn. She took to watching the Casey Affleck film *Manchester by the Sea*, an irrepressibly bleak movie about a man whose three young kids die in a house fire he is inadvertently responsible for. Birkin found a certain solace in it and liked to think that at least her losses of her father, mother, daughter, and Gainsbourg weren't *that* bad. She was chronically—likely terminally—ill and bereft, filled with regret, wondering if she should have been stricter during Kate's heady teenage years. It was the most difficult of all the deaths she had endured—she didn't think it was possible to overcome the death of a child. Something would always be missing, and everything would remind her of Kate. A nail clipper hanging off her Birkin bag would remind her of Kate's feet. A flower shop would no longer be associated with celebratory bouquets but rather with the cemetery where Kate was buried.

Birkin chose Montparnasse Cemetery for Kate's grave, just a few steps away from Serge Gainsbourg's plot, where fans often left cigarette butts and metro tickets as little offerings. The grave looks like a wild English garden transported to a stately Left Bank cemetery, where people might take a walk or go see a particularly ornate grave or find one of a favorite author or singer. One regular visitor to the cemetery wrote in her blog that she was walking through and saw Birkin, silent, lost in thought. She was tending to Kate's grave, a plastic bag filled with dried leaves and flowers, making sure her tiny plot looked just so. A young fan recognized her. She smiled, popped into a waiting taxi, and once again retreated into herself.

CHAPTER NINETEEN
Specters

After the death of Kate Barry, Jane Birkin was bereft. She stopped acting around 2014; she still toured, singing her old songs, but she needed to take her time with her devastation. She called Kate's death "the most important thing that had happened to me." Birkin spent seven years after the 2013 death not commenting on it, but she slowly started writing lyrics that addressed the loss. She told an interviewer, "I was listening to an old program on the radio yesterday, and they were asking Francis Bacon, 'Don't you find that your paintings are terribly violent?' And he said, 'Well, not half as violent as life.' And I thought, He's right," she said. "When people say, 'How can you write about how you found your daughter dead?,' well, it's nothing in comparison to finding your daughter dead."

She channeled her grief into a new project, *Oh! Pardon tu dormais . . .* (*Oh! Sorry You Were Sleeping*), which came out at the end of 2020, when Birkin was seventy-four. It was her fourteenth studio album and the first time she had written lyrics in English. The album spoke in a frank and unvarnished way about sorrow. The lyrics took on the rage she found in grief. "Cigarettes," most transparently, grapples with the deep impact of Kate's death and the absence of closure around why it happened. Birkin's nihilistic lyrics are set to a waltz, making for an especially unsettling effect. Birkin told *Vogue* that, for her writing process, she focused on anecdotes "that make things real."

Just like in her autobiographical film *Boxes*, Birkin used the theme of ghosts for *Oh! Pardon tu dormais . . .* One song is literally called "Ghosts" and speaks of the specters of death around her: daughter, mother, father, grandmother, grandfather, husband, nephew (her brother Andrew's son Anno died in 2001 at age twenty in a car accident), friends, dogs, and cats. In the album's last song, "Catch Me if You Can," she seemed to be speaking once again directly to the dead, perhaps Gainsbourg or Kate, saying that she was almost gone from view. This time she was preparing herself to join them. The inspiration for the song had come from a Post-it Birkin found on Kate's diary after her death that read "Happy as Ulysses between his parents." She wondered if that was what happened in the afterlife: that one was safe and rejoining their parents. It gave her some small sense of comfort.

Oh! Pardon tu dormais . . . got her some of the best reviews of her career. As an artist who had rarely received much appraisal outside the French-speaking world, she was given serious due. "Her latest compositions are in line with the sonic traditions she pioneered a half-century ago, but suffused with the darkly tinted wisdom of a life entering its winter," wrote the *Washington Post*. *Pitchfork* compared it to late-period masterpieces by musicians who were taken much more seriously by the critical establishment: Bob Dylan's *Rough and Rowdy Ways*, David Bowie's *Blackstar*, and Marianne Faithfull's *Negative Capability*. "*Oh! Pardon tu dormais . . .* is weary but never resigned, battle-scarred but never defeated, a work of personal reckoning marked by a frantic desire to connect, as our time slips away. None of us can cheat death; but to face it with Birkin's fortitude and poetic skill is to score a minor victory," wrote the *Pitchfork* critic.

Birkin agreed to participate in another documentary about her life, *Jane by Charlotte*, which turned out to be her last feature appearance. The film was Charlotte Gainsbourg's directorial debut. It follows the two of them, and occasionally Charlotte's daughter Alice, from 2017 to 2021 as Birkin was touring in Japan, New York, and back in France. She was performing—sometimes with Charlotte—from her last album of Serge Gainsbourg's music, 2017's *Birkin/Gainsbourg: Le symphonique*, featuring orchestral versions of his songs, and singing songs from *Oh! Pardon tu dormais . . .*

The film is intimate. The audience can see Birkin's aging face and body up close on the big screen—her veins, her liver spots, the glasses she needs to wear—alongside the more glamorous touches of her life, such as a Cartier tank watch or a tuxedo jacket. She now found her Birkin bag too heavy, so she started wearing oversize men's corduroy pants with big pockets or Carhartt work pants. She said to an interviewer in jest, "I would love to make a line of my own of really rather large corduroy trousers for large middle-aged ladies that could make them look slim."

Much of the documentary takes place in greenrooms of famed concert halls and five-star hotel rooms because Birkin was largely living on the road, even if her health was in decline. Sometimes she had to wear a morphine patch while she performed; sometimes she had to be helped onstage. She performed songs from *Le symphonique* for two years, playing with different symphony orchestras around the world.

The title of the movie is a conscious echo of the Agnès Varda documentary, positioning itself as a sort of sequel. But unlike the genre-bending creativity of *Jane B. par Agnès V.*, the dialogue between the filmmaker and the subject feels strained, even if the settings are familial: Birkin's home, a visit to a bulldog breeder, Birkin's first trip back to Serge Gainsbourg's home, which has been left untouched.

"It smells the same," she says on-camera. "It's almost like being in a dream." She remarked that rue des Saints-Pères, a street perpendicular to rue de Verneuil, is like the mythological river Styx. "I don't cross it. Everything that happened there seems to be from another time. As if this life belonged to another person. It's strange."

Birkin didn't find making a film with her daughter a particularly easy experience. "I wanted to stop. I didn't know what she wanted to get at. I didn't like the questions," she said. "So we took a year or two off. Then we met in New York and I realized she wasn't getting at anything. She needed answers to certain questions. . . . I hope she got the answers she wanted."

The discomfort comes across onscreen. Charlotte, Birkin said, "is a very mysterious person to me, so it was a way for her to . . . Well, it's her idea to get to know me. . . . I think she found out things she wanted to know." It is a surprisingly cold answer, but the documentary highlights an unexpected timidity, even an awkwardness, between mother and daughter. Despite how bold both Birkin and Charlotte were artistically, the documentary seems to explore the distance between them emotionally without quite saying that's the purpose. Charlotte has more than a bit of an anxious air about her, and Birkin seems so lost in her own often misguided optimism that they just cannot connect.

Charlotte said the theme of the film was a daughter looking for her mother, which is accurate but doesn't mean it was an artistic success. She "might have made the film for no one but herself," one *New York Times* critic said, characterizing it as "a meandering and elusive documentary portrait." A *Variety* review called it "sloppy," "casual/clumsy," and "amateurish," taking particular offense at the sound quality, and declaring that it "hardly qualifies as a movie."

Birkin participated in the movie both as a favor to her daughter and, as on her album, to ruminate on the past. In *Jane by Charlotte*, she is shown asking herself whether she had done a good or even adequate job as a mother. "Perhaps I wasn't responsible enough," she says at one point. Birkin worried that, in the years following Kate's death, she had been so wrapped up in her own distress that she didn't think of her children who were alive; that she glorified Kate. She admits she spent sleepless nights wondering what it meant to have put three beings into the world: Who would die, and when, and how? Her own mortality was clearly at the top of her mind. "And the fact that I won't be there to comfort you, that I'll be gone. I put you in orbit only to abandon you," she says, and then adds almost offhandedly that she needs to put everything in the girls' names for the purposes of taxes and duties.

Birkin attended Cannes for the premiere of *Jane by Charlotte* in May 2021 and then toured *Oh! Pardon tu dormais*... that summer. She was supposed to support the documentary that fall on the festival circuit, including the annual Deauville American Film Festival in September. Those plans were canceled because of her health. She had been on the beach with Gabrielle Crawford and complained of not feeling well. She fell, and after she got back to her feet, she was suffering from symptoms like headache, dizziness, and confusion. They took a taxi to a hospital in Nantes, where she had an emergency CAT scan that revealed a heavy brain hemorrhage and a stroke. Her family put out a statement in early September.

Her doctors advised her she needed a long rest. She canceled concert dates and took time off but hated the in-patient clinic where she was supposed to recover. She was in poor shape; she could barely see on one side, and that affected her balance. She was bored and she was angry at her body. She stayed for three weeks and checked herself out to go home; her house had been converted into a mini hospital with medical beds and wheelchairs. Crawford noticed that she popped morphine pills like candy. Birkin claimed she was just going to stay in and read Proust's *In Search of Lost Time*. Instead, after a week, she went out to cafés; after two weeks, she was out going to the movies; after three weeks, she went to see plays; and after a little over a month, she was onstage again. Her medical team had warned her that she was at a huge risk of pulmonary embolism from traveling and being in airplanes in her physical state, but she toured again, playing Beffroi de Montrouge, an art deco–era concert hall just outside Paris, in March 2022 (it was recorded as a live album and released a year later, memorialized as one of her last performances) and London's Barbican in July of that year.

Birkin had never seemed to live beyond her means, and her surviving daughters had busy careers, so choosing to perform in her final days was not a financial imperative. Putting her weakened body through extensive worldwide touring, which would have been taxing on even the healthiest person, was nearly masochistic. But that shows the autonomy she found late in life via performing:

a combination of passion for the songs, connection with her fans, and distraction from the reality of declining health with age. Touring was hard on her body, but it kept her spirits alive. She wanted her songs to be her final creative work. The stage had gone from a place that made her nervous to the last place she felt at home.

CHAPTER TWENTY

Your Jane B.

By late 2022 and early 2023, neighbors would report spotting Birkin in cafés or walking her dog. She took comfort in getting a coffee and a croissant in the morning, going to the Sunday organic farmers market on the boulevard Raspail, and spending time with her children and grandchildren. The French have a word, *flâneur*, that was popularized in the nineteenth century. It doesn't have an exact translation, but it's someone who walks around and hangs out, the kind of strolling that happens without errands or a fixed destination. Paris is a city for the *flâneur* and that was something Birkin always loved about it. She would eat *jambon beurre*, ham and butter sandwiches on baguettes, at Pont des Arts near the Louvre. From there, she liked to walk to the Jardin des Plantes, where there is a botanical garden, a natural history museum, and a zoo. Across the street at the Mosquée de Paris she could order mint tea in the courtyard café. The city was freedom for her. (In fact, she loved Paris so much that in 1992 she told Princess Diana that she should come live there, where the press would surely leave her alone.)

But by 2023, Birkin's public appearances were increasingly rare. She attended the César Awards in February 2023, walking the red carpet with Charlotte Gainsbourg and her granddaughter Alice Attal. Her eyes were bright but she looked ill, her face bloated, and her body held like she was in pain. In May 2023 she canceled concerts due to poor health. "Jane had been unwell for a long time, but she never stopped wanting to find expression. She kept pushing herself to the limit, however she was feeling, always there performing for those who loved her," said Charlotte Rampling. Without the ability to visit her usual haunts or spend a day making her way around the city, her quality of life suffered.

What made life worth living was certainly something Birkin had on her mind. "Before, when I was asked how I wanted to die, I would answer: 'The first.' Alas, life has decided otherwise. We are all a little scared of death when we feel it approaching. The idea is so distant, so abstract. We have trouble imagining it," said Birkin. "Over the last three years, I have come close to it twice, and, surprisingly, I didn't panic. I was more frightened of not having time to say what I wanted to say, to leave things in order, to be forgiven."

Her best friend, Gabrielle Crawford, held her hand while she was in the hospital or at home, but that was the only physical contact she wanted. In the spring of 2023, she said that she would like to marry Crawford, who thought she probably wanted to end her life with someone she had always loved and trusted. Birkin had even taken to signing her text messages to her best friend with "wife," a playful nod to a friendship that had lasted a lifetime and longer than their various romantic relationships.

Birkin had round-the-clock caregivers after her stroke in September 2021. In July 2023, Birkin asked to spend a night at home by herself. The next day, July 16, her body was found by a caregiver coming in for her shift. There was no trace of a struggle. "The first evening alone turned out to be her last. She had decided it," read a statement released by her family. Even though the word "suicide" was never mentioned, "she decided it" seems to imply that she chose to die on her own terms after battling illness for decades. "We don't know. I didn't need details. They hadn't helped us when Kate died," Crawford wrote in her memoir. Birkin hadn't wanted doctors or an ambulance to come. Instead, she had told her assistant to send everyone—her daughters, Crawford, everyone—away. "Then sitting at the oak table where, for forty years, she had received those she loved, alone she had gone," wrote Crawford. Birkin had been sick for fifteen years and her friends and family had all known this moment was inevitable, but her death was unexpected for all of them. Even worse, Birkin's home was burglarized right after she died, by people who used an iron bar to get in while Crawford was staying inside. The media picked up the story, which was another unwanted intrusion.

Jane Birkin's funeral was held on Monday, July 24, at the Église Saint-Roch, the same Left Bank church where Kate Barry's funeral had been held about a decade earlier. Among those in attendance were her surviving daughters Charlotte Gainsbourg and Lou Doillon, both looking tired and drawn but elegant in black suits. Serge Gainsbourg's son Lucien attended with his mother, Bambou (for whom he had bought a Birkin bag of her own). Famous friends such as Catherine Deneuve and her daughter Chiara Mastroianni, Isabelle Huppert, Charlotte Rampling, and Vanessa Paradis all attended, as did the French first lady Brigitte Macron and Culture Minister Rima Abdul Malak.

The funeral resembled something that would be held for a head of state. Access to the service inside the church was just for close friends and family, but there was a large screen set up outside for the hundreds of people who had shown up, carrying banners ("Merci Jane," "Jane Forever") and flowers that almost completely covered the square outside the church. Fans told journalists that they had "come to pay tribute to our little Englishwoman."

Inside Église Saint-Roch, Lou stood before the crowd and spoke to her mother directly: "Mum, thank you for all these adventures; thank you for not being ordinary, reasonable, or docile. This world of tomorrow, very peaceful and reasoned . . . it already bothers me."

Charlotte spoke of the fact that she now had no surviving father or mother. "I thank my father for loving my mother so much. And I thank my mother for loving him so much. I find myself an orphan. I see all your souls in pain without her. I already see the void she leaves us. It's my mom, it's our mom, his Jeanette, your Jane B."

As the pallbearers walked out, Birkin's 1983 song "Fuir le bonheur de peur qu'il ne se sauve" ("Running Away from Happiness lest It Run Away") was played. It was a respectful choice, not just for the lyrical content but for how she felt about her artistic trajectory.

"Until I was about thirty, I wasn't required to do much more than turn up. After that, my career got more interesting," she had said of her music some years earlier.

It was fitting for her to be buried in the Left Bank, in the city she had lived in for more than four decades. Once someone had asked her why she thought the French had welcomed her so openly. It was uncharacteristic of the national character to adopt a British woman with so much eagerness. "I fell in love with Serge, madly, then with them. I was adopted, and am still paying back that unexpected love," she said. Obituaries and appreciations were written in publications around the world, most focusing on her famous relationships, her famous children, and the famous bag that bore her name. "Singer, Actress, Fashion Inspiration," read the *New York Times* headline.

When Birkin was a child, her father had said of her favorite stuffed toy, "Maybe when we get to heaven it will be your monkey that greets us with open arms!" She had buried it with Serge Gainsbourg in 1991, but Birkin ended up close by. She was buried in Montparnasse Cemetery, sharing the same overgrown English secret garden of a plot with her daughter Kate. Fans still leave tokens for Birkin: miniature bulldog figurines, headshots of her, notes thanking her, bouquets of yellow mimosa, and shells.

Jane Birkin's last filmed performance was recorded in winter 2023 and came out a few months later in June 2023. In it, she sings "Jane B." alongside Franco-Belgian cellist Camille Thomas. Thomas is in a studio playing her cello, and Birkin is inside a glass vocal booth, wearing small wire-rim glasses, some wine-colored lipstick, and an oversize turtleneck sweater. The visual of an aging Birkin walled off from her fellow performer looks particularly isolating and lonely.

Sometimes pairing a pop song with a classical instrument feels like an easy trick, one to manipulate listeners to feel like the music is more meaningful than it is. In this case, at this late juncture in Birkin's life, the combination of the cello and Birkin's frailer-than-usual vocals ends up being genuinely moving.

Birkin used to joke that her last song would be "Je t'aime . . . moi non plus" for its notoriety, but she turned out to be wrong. It was "Jane B." There she was at seventy-six, still with bangs, singing a song her late partner wrote to introduce her to the world. The lyrics were unchanged, but the impact of hearing her sing about her younger self, age twenty or twenty-one, is profoundly sad. She is not trying to re-create her younger self; rather, she is singing, as a dying woman, an elegy to the life she led. And what an utterly fascinating life—one of great highs and lows, full of both infamy and impact—that could belong only to Jane B.

EPILOGUE

No one can dictate how they will be remembered after they die, but Jane Birkin at least had an idea of what her legacy might look like. Her persona was irresistible: a heady mix of openness, vulnerability, and freedom. She appeared to move through the world with so little friction that she executed a perfect magic trick: She made living a life as complex as hers seem wholly achievable to anyone.

Whether or not living like Birkin is actually possible for most, at least we can dress like her. She radiated an inner confidence and a knowingness nowhere more evident than through the way she dressed. Birkin's message, via style, was always so clear that her sartorial influence is one that exists beyond her. She was aware, mostly through her children, that the internet considered her a fashion icon: that there were popular photos of her, mostly in her early twenties, circulating to a flurry of likes and engagement on sites like Instagram (which she pronounced the French way, ahn-stah-grahm).

She was a product of her time, surely—someone so unbreakably representative of the 1960s and '70s—but she was also timeless. Even her own signature looks over the decades were dynamic and ever-evolving. As celebrated as they were, she didn't just indelibly shape the way women in her sphere of influence dressed in the '60s and '70s, but did so *twice* in her lifetime. Birkin was not content to be static, nor was she seemingly dressing for anyone but instead for her own happiness and comfort. She relayed a powerful message through clothes about who she was. So forgoing the crochet mini-dresses and Mary Janes she was known for at twenty-one years old was not about defeat but rather a sign of growth, of autonomy. She changed her style as she settled into middle age, wearing a black tuxedo to a state dinner at age forty-five and adopting a daily uniform of men's corduroys and oversize white cotton shirts in her fifties. All of it is not just worn today, but looks relevant on everyone. The same person could wear a sheer minidress while out dancing one night and bathe themselves in oversize menswear-inspired classics the next.

The concept of Jane Birkin shaped an aesthetic shorthand. "Jane Birkin" has become synonymous with a carefree and bourgeois-bohemian look. But plenty of famous people have become shorthand for a style or look. Birkin went far beyond that when her name took off without her. In a press release for a product called Nabila K Botanical Best Collagen and Biotin Conditioner, it is mentioned as good for use on tousled, just-off-center "Birkin bangs." Gwyneth Paltrow wrote that her company Goop's Colorblur balms are "a little Jane Birkin, a little New England summer ease." It is certainly ironic that an Englishwoman had such a large role in creating the modern French girl look. The same non sequitur channeling of Francophilia also fuels the popularity of brands that aren't at all French yet still have names such as Glossier, Comme Si, Agent Provocateur, Ouai, French Girl Organics, and on and on.

And then there is the $15,000 elephant in the room, or whatever the price of an entry-level Birkin bag is, should anyone be lucky enough to get their hands on one. The bag she couldn't escape. The Birkin is regarded today as a symbol of having made it for the nouveau riche: most Real Housewives and Kardashian-Jenners, as well as Victoria Beckham, have them; the musician Drake has a significant collection he has amassed as a kind of dowry for a future wife. Due to the popularity of the brand Telfar's Shopping Bag with creative types, particularly among people of color and within the queer community, it was dubbed the Bushwick Birkin. Even the nonchalant, verging on abusive way Jane wore her own Birkins, with trinkets draped all over them, became its own trend when social media influencers began to show how to "Birkinify" one's bag or even one's phone with similar charms to show personality and lack of fuss. "Birkin" has also become shorthand for the ultimate or most expensive. A plastic surgeon, Dr. Ryan Neinstein, called his $75,000 body lift from the neck to the knees, which requires nearly bisecting the waist, the Birkin Body. Birkin had a very healthy, very dry, very dark sense of humor. She *might* have been able to find the humor in it.

Birkin the individual, though, was a cult figure, not a symbol of mass culture, particularly outside of France. She was an icon, yes. But being regarded as an icon is different from being creatively revered. Certainly, her music was beloved. Few French-language songs, let alone rock-inflected ones, cross over into other countries or have any lasting historical impact. "Je t'aime . . . moi non plus" did and was covered by artists from Donna Summer to Giorgio Moroder to Pet Shop Boys. Birkin's biggest English-language roles were in Agatha Christie ensembles in the late 1970s, so in her native United Kingdom and in the United States she was obscure. Most people in the English-speaking world didn't know she worked as an actress and singer until her death. Fame did not preoccupy her, but her legacy has been co-opted by the popular culture in a way that she might not have fathomed.

It was a different time. That is an easy way to contextualize so much of Jane Birkin's life; a way to shrug off the beats of her story that didn't age well or feel uncomfortable in retrospect. That includes her relationships with older or domineering men and staying out at nightclubs all night, coming home at dawn, and then dropping her daughters off to school before finally going to sleep. Birkin was inclined to agree, saying three years before she died, in 2020, "To even imagine my youth, I don't know. It was another time." But we cannot consider her choices solely as a product of her times.

To dig into her life, parts that didn't age well and all, is to understand that she engaged in a pattern of behavior when it came to relationships. She sought out a very particular type of love: one that was dizzying with a roller coaster of emotional highs and lows. When describing her concept of romance, the word that I keep coming back to is "adolescent." She got her first taste of fame around the same time she got her first taste of dating. She spent the rest of her life chasing that same cocktail of feelings, and throughout Birkin's life—from her twenties into her sixties—she continued to be overly idealistic in relationships, sought out the kinds of operatic emotions that inspire one to write dramatic poetry, and again and again chose to align herself with a specific kind of romantic partner.

Birkin will be remembered for her proximity to volatile men, most notably Serge Gainsbourg, John Barry, and Jacques Doillon. Time after time, she chose men who were older, who had more power, who had more artistic freedom than she did. And besides her romantic partners, Birkin was unabashedly friendly with many figures who were caught up in scandals about sex, power, and agency: Gérard Depardieu, Woody Allen, Roman Polanski.

In an interview with CNN in 2020, Birkin talked about the difference in sexual mores between France and America and Britain. France is "usually about ten years behind England and maybe fifteen years behind America in the drive to speak out against sexual misbehavior," she said. France is a country that prides itself on maintaining its libertine predispositions, especially ones that were so deeply informed by the May '68 generation that Birkin was a part of. But the values of that time period have continued to plague French society, with actors, directors, and literary figures all accused of inappropriate relationships, particularly with underage girls.

France experienced its own #MeToo reckoning, albeit with a different trajectory than its American counterpart, which Birkin bore witness to. Catherine Deneuve, the grande dame of French cinema, was one of a hundred women who signed a 2018 open letter accusing the #MeToo campaign of being too reactionary. "We defend a right to pester, which is vital to sexual freedom," the statement said. This is, of course, a reductive way of seeing gender relations, as if it's a zero-sum game where a woman's right not to be harassed directly takes away from men's virility. Birkin didn't sign the letter, but she also didn't disagree with it: "I know for a fact that Deneuve is a feminist who sticks up for other women. I think she was defending men's right to flirt. But she was probably unwise to sign a letter with other people who are rather dubious," she said.

In 2020, the Portuguese-Belgian singer Lio, who was fifty-eight at the time, told a radio show, "I have gone off Gainsbourg, who is quite simply a harasser." She said that he was "not cool with girls" and called him "a Weinstein of songs in a certain way." Lio wasn't the only person who wanted the country to reevaluate the legacy of one of its most famous voices. An op-ed in the French magazine *Philosophie* asked "why a man who in theory checks every box to be 'canceled' still hasn't been." Birkin left Serge Gainsbourg in 1981, but because she was so closely associated with him, and because she was never one to shy away from speaking about anything in public, she responded to Lio's accusations. She maintained a kind of plausible deniability because she'd left him decades before. But she also defended him. "I don't think it equated with the Serge that any of us knew," Birkin told *The Times* (London). "I know perfectly well that he wasn't that sort of person. I think he was saying exactly what he thought. . . . You can't judge things by other epoques, you can't measure them by this extraordinary state that Me Too has made. . . . He was a very honest man, so he had a tendency to say exactly what he thought. If on top of it he was plastered, even more so." Over ten thousand people signed a petition to prevent a stop on the Paris metro being named in his honor, calling him a "violent man, a notorious misogynist, and a champion of incest." The Serge Gainsbourg station on the 11 line linking Châtelet to Rosny-Bois-Perrier opened in summer 2024.

The men with whom Birkin aligned herself with right up until the end of her life continued to be part of the debate in France around sexual politics. In 2024, the actress Judith Godrèche, at the age of fifty-one, said she had been abused by two French directors as a minor. The first was Benoît Jacquot, who she said had groomed and sexually assaulted her when he was thirty-nine and she was fourteen. The other was a more familiar name: Jacques Doillon. He was accused of sexually abusing her when she was fifteen. More specifically, that Doillon had her do forty-five takes of an unscripted sex scene with him during the shooting of his 1989 film *La fille de*

15 ans (*The 15 Year Old Girl*), which was during his partnership with Birkin. He cited these as false accusations in a statement. He was questioned but released without charges being filed and denied the claims.

It is beyond the scope of this book to litigate the actions or accusations against Birkin's partners. She should not be punished for her taste in men, nor should she be held accountable for their actions. The discussion around her choice of men—be they friends or romantic partners—should not be judgmental but rather focus on how they invariably shaped her career and her life. Gainsbourg, Doillon, and Barry should not be a stain on Birkin's legacy and instead absorbed into a story of a woman who was attracted to genius almost to the point of overlooking her own ambition—and their behavior. Nonetheless she did eventually take on her own image. Not by summiting some mountain of empowerment where she was finally free from complicated relationships and critically appreciated by all—that isn't the real world, even for someone like her, who led such a singular and charming life.

So what *did* preoccupy Jane Birkin? What did a woman whose default public face was happy-go-lucky actually spend her time and energy chasing? She was certainly ambitious, but her driving force was not naked ambition. Rather it was the kind that developed alongside her own creative and personal evolution. She wanted artistic success and respect from her peers, but she was never going to move beyond her own comfort zone to win big awards or become a huge draw at the box office. She understood who she was, and she was happy to be seen as Jane Birkin, singing many of Gainsbourg's songs on tour, even if that meant becoming more and more of a nostalgic figure as the years went by. She didn't want to go too far afield or defy her own history because it fulfilled something in her—an enduring desire for a life filled with nostalgia and romance. What she was looking for was acknowledgment on her own terms.

That desire was met in the tribute concert *Jane Birkin by Friends* on February 3, 2024, about six months after her death in the summer of 2023. The backstory was bittersweet. Before her death, Birkin had been scheduled to perform that night at L'Olympia de Paris—she had always wanted to be onstage, performing until the very end. Her manager had the idea to keep the date to re-create the night Birkin had planned: the same musicians and crew, the same set list in the same order, the same arrangements and production on songs. To perform the songs, they enlisted artists with close connections to Birkin: friends and collaborators like the actress Marion Cotillard, who sang "Jane B."; former French first lady Carla Bruni; Vanessa Paradis, the Gainsbourg protégée pop star and ex of Johnny Depp, who sang "Di doo dah" from Birkin's 1973 solo album; and Jarvis Cocker of the Britpop band Pulp. Her daughters Charlotte and Lou were there, both wearing black ensembles, looking not exactly happy but moved by the experience and grateful for the sold-out crowd of fans.

The night was a full-circle moment. After a lifetime of being defined by inspiring people, trying to defy her muse status, and watching it reverberate beyond her story, Birkin was celebrated for her own artistry. Finally, during this evening of tribute, she managed to escape the image of herself: It was about the music. That's the legacy—one of creation and selflessness—that she longed for.

Birkin's career does not neatly fit into one clearly defined box. She was more than the sum of all those parts. Seeing her as simply an inspirational figure flattens her. By the end of her life, she'd moved on from her role as a muse. She was a tastemaker who changed the world around her, altered the cultural fabric of the times with her artistry and individuality. The nature of her fame can only really be understood when it's viewed in its totality. She was a complex and flawed woman who navigated a web of ambitions, creativity, and relationships. Again and again, her image was taken away from her, and yet she worked to take it back and wrestle with her own history. It was not one outfit, one relationship, one song, or one role. Jane Birkin made herself real.

AUTHOR'S NOTE

Jane Birkin kept volumes of journals beginning when she was a child. Her personal writing was an invaluable way to track the events in her life, but, more than that, how her values and perspectives on the world changed over time. The journals invited me into her interior world, a place where she bloomed into existence in a way that forced me to recognize her complexities. The two published volumes of Jane Birkin's diaries, *Munkey Diaries* and *Post-Scriptum*, were essential for understanding her most intimate opinions and psychological states, but I kept in mind that they were diaries: Sometimes you turn to them at the height of an emotional moment or exaggerate what happened. There are entire years whose original entries went missing or were too damaged to decipher, so Birkin relied on her own memories to re-create them, such as a few entries undated in 1986 marking the timeline of Kate Barry's addiction.

Many famous anecdotes from her life have been told many times: in the diary, in interviews, by her brother or directors. And those accounts can differ each time—for example, the story of her jumping into the Seine, or who exactly arranged the first dinner with her and Serge Gainsbourg at Maxim's, or whether it was 1983 or 1984 when she boarded the flight that led to the creation of the Birkin bag. Birkin could be something of a fabulist when she recalled living down the street from where Edith Piaf died. That seemed to have been a construct of her imagination or some kind of conflation of crowds holding a vigil for Piaf, because while Piaf had lived on that same boulevard, she died in the South of France.

Regardless, Birkin wrote a letter home to her family that she could hear Piaf's voice from beyond the grave when she rode the elevator in her building. I remained highly aware of this as a biographer and fact-checked Birkin's memories and dates and compared them to outside sources whenever possible.

Jane Birkin lived a bilingual life. Nowhere is that more in evidence than in the diaries. They began in her native English and were written, after her fluency developed and her life in France became more permanent, in both English and French. *Munkey Diaries* was translated into English, and I quoted directly from that edition. *Post-Scriptum* was never translated into English, so I used the French edition and translated quotes into English myself.

I used this approach for all my research, whether it was articles, books, diaries, interviews, or films. When available, I quoted previous English translations, but otherwise I did my own translations. As for my own French-language ability, I studied it through high school and college and spent my last year of college at the University of Paris, immersed alongside native speakers at the Jussieu and Sorbonne campuses. My French is good, sometimes even great, but I am, like Birkin, not a native speaker.

The most pleasurable part of writing a book is research, and the scope of *It Girl* was vast, beyond the hundreds of interviews conducted and read, from watching a film series on May '68 cinema at Metrograph in New York City to visiting the Alaïa archives in Paris. They influenced this book even if they were not explicitly referenced.

I did not meet Jane Birkin during her lifetime, nor have I met her daughters or her extended family or close friends, including her sister, brother, and Gabrielle Crawford, who either declined to participate or did not respond to my requests for an interview. I frequently refer to them by their first names in this book not to be informal, but just to keep them from being confused with their fathers, who are generally identified, like everyone else in the book, by their last names.

ACKNOWLEDGMENTS

Many thanks are due to everyone who assisted me in this project, including my agent, Jen Marshall, and the team at Atria Books: Kate Napolitano, Falon Kirby, Zakiya Jamal, Debbie Norflus, Hannah Frankel, and Molly Burgoyne. I am also so grateful for the help of Julia Cheiffetz, Chelsea Fairless, Christina Frank, Kayla Grogan, Zoé Guédard, Jamie Johns, Faye Landes, Glynnis MacNicol, Rob Matthews, Octavia Peissel, Sarah Perks, Grace Robinson-Leo, Tara Timinsky, Allison Warren, and my parents, Alyson Kennedy and Paul Meltzer.

NOTES

INTRODUCTION

1 *Birkin . . . dumps out its contents*: Agnès Varda, dir., *Jane B. par Agnès V.*, 1988, clip posted on Instagram by @birkingainsbourgmusique, https://www.instagram.com/reel/CvUKpKfAhMy/?igshid=MzRlODBiNWFlZA%3D%3D.

3 *"Men often saw me as their B-side"*: Olivier Lalanne, "Jane Birkin sur la vie, l'amour, la mode et Serge Gainsbourg," *Vogue France*, July 16, 2023, https://www.vogue.fr/vogue-hommes/culture/story/interview-sans-filtre-avec-jane-birkin-sur-son-style-ses-amours-et-serge-gainsbourg/645?page=2.

4 *"a French icon"*: Ellie Iorizzo, "President Macron Describes Jane Birkin as 'French Icon' Following Death at 76," *Independent*, July 16, 2023, https://www.the-independent.com/news/uk/jane-birkin-emmanuel-macron-french-paris-president-b2376186.html.

4 *"the most Parisian of the English"*: Iorizzo, "President Macron Describes Jane Birkin."

4 Libération *wrote in her obituary*: Melanie Goodfellow, "Jane Birkin Dominates Front Pages as France Mourns Death of British Actress and Singer; President Declares Her a French Icon," *Deadline*, October 22, 2023, https://deadline.com/2023/07/jane-birkin-death-france-reaction-1235439588/.

CHAPTER ONE: ECCENTRIC, GLAMOROUS, AND ALL QUITE BRILLIANT

9 *"an intruder, disguised as our sister"*: Andrew Birkin, *Serge Gainsbourg et Jane Birkin: l'album de famille intime* (Paris: Éditions Albin Michel, 2022).

9 *"She had a taste for drama"*: Gabrielle Crawford, *C'est Jane, Birkin Jane* (Arles, France: Actes Sud, 2024).

9 *"She said I was lucky"*: Jason Solomons, "'Serge Needed All the Love He Could Get,'" *Guardian*, August 15, 2004, https://www.theguardian.com/music/2004/aug/15/popandrock1.

10 *they staged an original holiday play*: Jane Birkin, *Munkey Diaries: The Extraordinary Early Years of an International Icon* (London: Weidenfeld & Nicolson, 2021).

11 *"I spent three miserable, cowardly, sad, ordinary years"*: Birkin, *Munkey Diaries.*

12 *"I'm the same as everyone else"*: Birkin, *Munkey Diaries.*

12 *"'Are you Judy Campbell's daughter?'"*: Sarah Nechamkin, "Jane Birkin on Her Regrets, Romances, and Renewed Sense of Self," *Interview*, December 15, 2020, https://www.interviewmagazine.com/music/jane-birkin-interview.

13 *a poem called "Suicide Lost"*: Birkin, *Munkey Diaries.*

14 *she mentioned offhandedly in later interviews*: Beatrice Hazelhurst, "Jane Birkin's Legacy Lives On," *Paper*, January 29, 2018, https://www.papermag.com/jane-birkin-interview.

CHAPTER TWO: CAN'T YOU MAKE AN EFFORT?

16 *"if you send me to France, I'll kill myself!"*: Crawford, *C'est Jane, Birkin Jane.*

17 *"French women start with the same ingredients"*: Natasha Silva-Jelly, "Jane Birkin Opens Up About Her Ageless Style," *Harper's Bazaar*, January 25, 2018, https://www.harpersbazaar.com/culture/features/a15873144/jane-birkin-interview/.

19 *"You'd see photos of Julie Christie"*: Silva-Jelly, "Jane Birkin Opens Up."

20 *Sigmund Freud*: Susan Hiner, *Accessories to Modernity: Fashion and the Feminine in Nineteenth-Century France* (Philadelphia: University of Pennsylvania Press, 2010).

21 *"whether he thought I had a chance as an actress"*: Nechamkin, "Jane Birkin on Her Regrets."

22 *"one of Mr. Greene's favorite characters, God"*: Dan Sullivan, "The Theater: Graham Greene's 'Carving a Statue,'" *New York Times*, May 1, 1968, https://archive.nytimes.com/www.nytimes.com/books/00/02/20/specials/greene-carving.html.

22 *"Class of '65—50 Women to Keep an Eye On"*: Crawford, *C'est Jane, Birkin Jane.*

23 *"I thought he was very good-looking"*: Birkin, *Munkey Diaries.*

24 *"To her great disappointment, he never came"*: Crawford, *C'est Jane, Birkin Jane.*

24 *"I was brought up to think"*: Nechamkin, "Jane Birkin on Her Regrets."

25 *"There was such insecurity, it was quite crazy"*: Hannah Nathanson, "Jane Birkin on Chasing Beauty," *Elle* [UK], October 2020, up-

dated July 17, 2023, https://www.elle.com/uk/beauty/a34459195/jane-birkin-chasing-beauty/.

29 *"That place," he later told* Mojo: *Mojo*, June 1997.

CHAPTER THREE: FOLIE À DEUX

31 *"She described him as this ghastly man"*: Karin Nelson, "Serge Gainsbourg and Jane Birkin: A Family Affair," *W Magazine*, October 25, 2013, https://www.wmagazine.com/story/jane-birkin-serge-gainsbourg.

31 *"He did have quite a reputation in France"*: Rachel Brodsky, "Jane Birkin on Grief, Jealousy, and Her Most Personal Album Ever," *Stereogum*, February 4, 2021, https://www.stereogum.com/2114979/jane-birkin-oh-pardon-tu-dormais-interview/interviews/tracking-down/.

31 *"She was a girl of light, I, a man of shadow"*: *Elle* [France], July 20, 2023.

33 *the BBC reported in 1970*: "1970: Jane Birkin Interview | 24 Hours | Classic Interviews," posted July 20, 2023, by BBC Archive, YouTube, https://www.youtube.com/watch?v=xpyK_kbSIpY.

33 *"Equality for women doesn't exist"*: Gilles Verlant, *Gainsbourg: The Biography*, trans. Paul Knobloch (Los Angeles: TamTam Books, 2012).

35 *"I'd be a kind of Pygmalion to her"*: Verlant, *Gainsbourg: The Biography*.

36 *"It's like when you break a string on a guitar"*: Verlant, *Gainsbourg: The Biography*.

36 *"I was at his side the whole time"*: Verlant, *Gainsbourg: The Biography*.

39 *"We didn't think about May '68"*: Ludovic Perrin, "Jane Birkin: 'Serge Gainsbourg Was a Provocateur with a Wildly Romantic Soul,'" *Le Monde*, August 26, 2013, updated on September 6, 2023, https://www.lemonde.fr/en/culture/article/2023/07/17/jane-birkin-serge-gainsbourg-was-a-provocateur-with-a-wildly-romantic-soul_6055830_30.html.

40 *"struggling with her nemesis"*: Andrew Birkin, *Serge Gainsbourg et Jane Birkin*.

41 *"'Same room as usual, Mr. Gainsbourg?'"*: Jane Birkin, "Jane Birkin on Love and Loss," *Document Journal*, July 16, 2023, https://www.documentjournal.com/2016/12/jane-birkin-serge-gainsbourg/.

43 *"Serge treated me as an equal"*: Andrew Birkin, "Andrew Birkin Reflects on Swinging London, the Beatles and His Sister Jane in 'A Life in Pictures,'" *Variety*, March 20, 2022, https://variety.com/2022/film/news/beatles-jane-birkin-1235208066/.

43 *"My daughter came home and declared"*: Verlant, *Gainsbourg: The Biography*.

45 *"because of my basket and his ears"*: Lucy Brook, "Jane Birkin on Serge Gainsbourg and Paris in the 70s," *RUSSH*, July 16, 2023, https://www.russh.com/jane-birkin/.

45 *"others seem bland"*: @birkingainsbourgmusique, "Even his beauty. . . ." posted on Instagram December 30, 2022, https://www.instagram.com/p/CmyCUKSujZA/.

46 *Decades later, she said*: Nechamkin, "Jane Birkin on Her Regrets."

CHAPTER FOUR: IT'S LIKE SHE'S NOT ACTING AT ALL

52 *found her acting uninteresting*: Rebecca Nicholson, "Jane Birkin: 'I Learned French off a Tape Recorder. All the French People Laughed,'" *Guardian*, June 19, 2018, https://www.theguardian.com/lifeandstyle/2017/apr/22/jane-birkin-i-learned-french-off-a-tape-recorder.

52 *"She inspired jealousy, whereas I inspired friendliness"*: Lalanne, "Jane Birkin sur la vie."

CHAPTER FIVE: JE T'AIME . . . MOI NON PLUS

54 *"groans, sighs, and Bardot's little cries of pleasure"*: Sylvie Simmons, "The Eyes Have It," *Guardian*, February 2, 2001, https://www.theguardian.com/books/2001/feb/02/culture.features.

55 *"I was the figure of fun in the musical"*: Nechamkin, "Jane Birkin on Her Regrets."

56 *"At 21, Jane Birkin Has All the Luck"*: "Les Passagers du 83," *Jours de France*, January 1969.

56 *Birkin kissing Kate on the nose*: "Inséparables, Jane, Serge et Kate," *Jours de France*, no. 773, October 2, 1969, https://web.archive.org/web/20240619070345/http://www.exfandebirkin.com/pages/unes-fin-60.html#joursdefrance692.

56 *"The Englishwoman Who Was Conquered by Paris"*: Bernard Delmont, "Cette Anglaise que Paris a conquise mais qui a conquis Serge Gainsbourg," *La vie Parisienne*, October 1969.

56 *"World Famous in Three Minutes"*: "Nach drei Minuten weltberühmt," *Schweizer Illustrierte*, May 26, 1969.

56 *"The Bored Gazelle"*: "La gacela aburrida," *Siete Dias Ilustrados*, January 13–19, 1969.

56 *"Jane Proves the Language of Love Is Universal"*: Laurie Henshaw, "Jane Proves the Language of Love Is Universal," *Melody Maker*, August 23, 1969.

56 *A BBC report on Birkin and Gainsbourg*: "1970: Jane Birkin Interview," BBC Archive.

57 *"Erotic Record Shunned"*: Henshaw, "Jane Proves the Language of Love Is Universal."

57 *verboten*: *Pop*, December 1969.

57 *"Jane and I have this in common"*: "Jane Birkin et soudain ce fut la célébrité," *Le Soir Illustré*, October 2, 1969.

57 *"I don't know what all the fuss was about"*: Solomons, "'Serge Needed All the Love.'"

59 *"The Ugly Man I Love"*: *Weekend*, April 29–May 5, 1970, image posted by @addictedtorags, Instagram, https://www.instagram.com/addictedtorags/p/DG6croZyPhP/.

59 *"My true liberation"*: *Les Inrockuptibles*, October 23, 2019, excerpt posted by @birkingainsbourgmusique, Instagram, https://www.instagram.com/p/DIp7IeWgBIQ/.

59 *In an interview for* Slogan: "'Slogan' Interview (English Subtitles) Serge Gainsbourg/Jane Birkin," posted April 27, 2020, by Julia J, YouTube, https://www.youtube.com/watch?v=l5Dyxq2kw-c.

59 *"Her roles have a certain similarity"*: "1970: Jane Birkin Interview," BBC Archive.

59 *the French talk show* Variances: "Interviews croisées de Serge Gainsbourg et Jane Birkin—1970," November 9, 1970, https://www.ina.fr/ina-eclaire-actu/video/cpf11000025/interviews-croisees-de-serge-gainsbourg-et-jane-birkin.

CHAPTER SIX: NONCHALANCE PERSONIFIED

61 *an interview with the designer Jean Paul Gaultier*: Alexandra Marshall, "A Conversation with Jane Birkin in 2010," *An American Who Fled Paris* (blog), July 21, 2023, https://alexandramarshall.substack.com/p/a-conversation-with-jane-birkin-in.

62 *"The Emancipated Venus of the New Age"*: *Ciné Revue*, October 16, 1969.

62 Petticoat *magazine ran her makeup routine*: *Petticoat*, March 1968.

62 *devoted a whole story to "Jane's Basket"*: *Pariscope*, no. 291, November 22–28 (year unknown), https://web.archive.org/web/20230725185413/http://www.exfandebirkin.com/medias/images/pariscop.le.panier.de.jane.n-.291.22-28.novembre.jpg?fx=r_1200_800.

62 *she was once denied entry to the restaurant Maxim's*: Birkin, *Munkey Diaries*.

63 *"I will not prostitute my art"*: Alexander Fury, "In with the New: Balenciaga Announces Alexander Wang's Replacement, and You've

Probably Never Heard of Him," *Independent*, October 7, 2015, https://www.the-independent.com/life-style/fashion/in-with-the-new-balenciaga-announces-alexander-wang-s-replacement-and-you-ve-probably-never-heard-of-him-a6685136.html.

64 *"I don't care much about expensive couture clothes"*: Claude de Leusse, "Girl of Today," *Women's Wear Daily*, August 19, 1969.

64 *"I think I've got it"*: *Le Figaro*, April 2014, posted by @birkingainsbourgmusique, Instagram, https://www.instagram.com/birkingainsbourgmusique/p/DGwn-ViAHqb/?img_index=1.

66 *the night was "a giggle"*: Sarah Hyde, "The Rothschilds 1971 Costume Ball, Honouring Marcel Proust," *World of Interiors*, December 5, 2022, https://www.worldofinteriors.com/story/proust-ball.

67 *in a French television interview*: "Serge Gainsbourg's Paris Home to Open to the Public—Ashtrays Still Brimming," France 24, April 3, 2023, https://www.france24.com/en/france/20230403-serge-gainsbourg-s-paris-home-to-open-to-the-public-%E2%80%93-ashtrays-still-brimming.

67 *"Daydreaming and melancholy are my drugs"*: Lucien Rioux, March 1968, posted by @birkingainsbourgmusique, Instagram, https://www.instagram.com/birkingainsbourgmusique/p/Cpg2I2bNd_U/.

CHAPTER SEVEN: WE ARE AN AMORAL COUPLE

74 *covered in pop culture magazines like* Paris Jour: *Paris Jour*, no. 3587, March 26, 1971, https://web.archive.org/web/20160617130108/http://www.exfandebirkin.com/medias/images/jane-birkin-et-serge-gainsbourg-couverture-paris-jour-n-3587-vendredi-26-mars-1971.jpg.

74 *"Maternité = Mariage"*: "Gainsbourg et Birkin: maternité = marriage," https://web.archive.org/web/20160617133024/http://www.exfandebirkin.com/medias/images/jane-birkin-et-serge-gainsbourg-bonne-soiree-1971-3.jpg.

75 *"entirely Kate"*: Andrew Birkin, *Serge Gainsbourg et Jane Birkin*.

75 *skintight blue sequined dress*: Elizabeth Day, "Interview: Charlotte Gainsbourg, the Daughter of Serge and Jane Birkin, on Her Wild Childhood and Her Sister's Death," *Times* (London), November 12, 2017.

76 *"Over time, it all faded away"*: *Hep Taxi!*, 2021, posted by @birkingainsbourgmusique, Instagram, https://www.instagram.com/birkingainsbourgmusique/p/DGuGBr3AMFr/.

CHAPTER EIGHT: I CHUCKED MYSELF INTO THE SEINE

82 *"Its premise is a tad out of left field"*: Glenn Kenny, "'Je t'aime moi non plus' Review: Serge Gainsbourg's Oddball Directorial Debut," *New York Times*, October 11, 2019, https://www.nytimes.com/2019/10/10/movies/je-taime-moi-non-plus-review.html.

83 *"I was a kind of object"*: Judith Perrignon, "'I Was a Kind of Object and That's What I Wanted to Be': Jane Birkin, from 1969 to #MeToo," *Le Monde*, July 18, 2023, https://www.lemonde.fr/en/m-le-mag/article/2023/07/18/i-was-a-kind-of-object-and-that-s-what-i-wanted-to-be-jane-birkin-from-1969-to-metoo_6057967_117.html.

CHAPTER NINE: EX FAN DES SIXTIES

90 *"she took it on the chin with me"*: Véronique Mortaigne, *Je T'aime: The Legendary Love Story of Jane Birkin and Serge Gainsbourg*, trans. Georg Philipp von Pezold (London: Icon Books, 2019).

92 *"The Mysterious 'Divorce'"*: "The Mysterious 'Divorce' of Serge Gainsbourg and Jane Birkin," *France Dimanche*, October 1980.

92 Paris Match *ran a photo*: Jean Noli, "Serge and Jane: La fin d'un amour de 12 ans," *Paris Match*, October 24, 1980.

CHAPTER TEN: THE NEW JANE

93 *"I was suddenly allowed to go ballistic on screen"*: Lalanne, "Jane Birkin sur la vie."

94 *"I knew that if I jumped, he would be there to receive me"*: David Hudson, "The Steely Fragility of Jane Birkin," Criterion, July 18, 2023, https://www.criterion.com/current/posts/8205-the-steely-fragility-of-jane-birkin.

95 *during a retrospective of her work*: "Jane Birkin et Jacques Doillon, une leçon de cinéma," Cinémathèque Française, February 4, 2017, https://www.cinematheque.fr/video/991.html.

95 *"New Jane"*: "La Nouvelle Jane Birkin," *Première*, April 1981.

95 *"Jane Birkin Starts a New Life"*: *Le Soir Illustré*, April 30, 1981.

95 *learning to smile again*: Anne Chabrol, "Jane Birkin recommence à sourire," *Elle*, April 1981.

96 *"my face didn't match it"*: Hélène Mathieu, "Jane Birkin: Épanouie-moi? Jamais!," *Marie Claire*, July 1984.

96 *"a new Jane Birkin, inhabiting her physicality"*: Elisabeth Vincentelli, "Jane Birkin: An Adventurous Artist Made in England, Forged in France," *New York Times*, July 18, 2023, https://www.nytimes.com/2023/07/16/arts/music/jane-birkin-french-icon.html.

CHAPTER ELEVEN: A NEWBORN, A SCHOOLGIRL, AND A TEEN

98 *"He took it so well yesterday"*: Jane Birkin, *Post-Scriptum: Journal, 1982–2013* (Paris: Librairie Arthème Fayard, 2019).

100 *"He was so essential in our lives"*: Lisa Robinson, "The Secret World of Serge Gainsbourg," *Vanity Fair*, October 15, 2007, https://www.vanityfair.com/news/2007/11/gainsbourg200711?srsltid=AfmBOooLAHN2AHacTc8jjkusYjcU5hoDpurBAZS-FdE1Kp2UfMEWvIRi.

102 *"I went into a tailspin"*: Crawford, *C'est Jane, Birkin Jane*.

104 *"a drunkard like my father"*: Kim Willsher, "Life, Death and Serge: Jane Birkin Reveals Her Insecurities in Emotional Memoir," *Guardian*, October 27, 2019, https://www.theguardian.com/culture/2019/oct/27/jane-birkin-serge-gainsbourg-emotional-memoir.

104 *Charlotte Gainsbourg said of her father in* Vanity Fair: Robinson, "The Secret World of Serge Gainsbourg."

105 *"people went to see her out of curiosity"*: Sheila Johnston, "The New Wave Rebels," *Guardian*, July 3, 1986.

106 *"I think the point with 'Lemon Incest'"*: Ed Potton, "Jane Birkin on the Truth About Serge Gainsbourg and the Pain of Her Daughter's Death," *Times* (London), December 11, 2020, https://www.thetimes.com/article/jane-birkin-interview-her-new-album-the-truth-about-serge-gainsbourg-and-the-pain-of-her-daughters-death-5l62c5qhh.

107 *"I look at it now and I see how uncomfortable I look"*: Robinson, "The Secret World of Serge Gainsbourg."

107 *"I understood . . . that people have desires"*: James Mottram, "Charlotte Gainsbourg: A French Affair," *Independent*, April 28, 2006, https://www.independent.co.uk/news/people/profiles/charlotte-gainsbourg-a-french-affair-6102410.html.

108 *Charlotte would later play down the whole episode*: Arwa Mahdawi, "Charlotte Gainsbourg: 'Everything Now Is So Politically Correct. So Boring,'" *Guardian*, October 31, 2019, https://www.theguardian.com/culture/2019/oct/26/charlotte-gainsbourg-everything-now-so-politically-correct-boring.

CHAPTER TWELVE: THE ME AND THE I

111 *"I was trying to invent a new category"*: Kevin Thomas, "Agnes Varda: Controversy in Eye of Beholder," June 22, 1989, https://www.latimes.com/archives/la-xpm-1989-06-22-ca-2869-story.html.

112 *"The people I loved . . . being a bit bossy"*: Michèle Manceaux, "Entrez dans ma maison," *Marie Claire*, May 1988.

113 *"This might be your last chance"*: Allison P. Davis, "A Film Retro-

spective Pays Tribute to the Chicest Mother-Daughter Duo," The Cut, January 29, 2016, https://www.thecut.com/2016/01/jane-birkin-film-retrospective.html.

114 *"Such a Lolita, I didn't want to do that anymore"*: Davis, "A Film Retrospective."

114 *Gainsbourg . . . wanted to be unseen by fans*: Crawford, *C'est Jane, Birkin Jane.*

114 *continuing on her creative trajectory*: Nicholson, "Jane Birkin: 'I Learned French off a Tape Recorder.'"

115 *"all the charm of her smelly gym socks"*: Caryn James, "She's 40. He's 15. Hmmm," *New York Times*, June 23, 1989, https://www.nytimes.com/1989/06/23/movies/review-film-she-s-40-he-s-15-hmmm.html.

115 *the critic Roger Ebert wrote*: Kevin Thomas, "Agnès Varda: Controversy in Eye of Beholder," *Los Angeles Times*, June 22, 1989.

CHAPTER THIRTEEN: BIRKIN LIKE THE BAG

121 *"We were the only people on the sidewalk"*: Stacey Vanek Smith, "With the Birkin Bag, Hermès Plays Hard to Get," NPR, December 31, 2015, https://www.npr.org/transcripts/460870534.

121 *since the value of a Birkin doubles about every five years*: Jasmine Li, "Birkin Bags Can Double in Value in 5 Years. An Hermès Expert Explains Why It's a Better Investment Than Gold," *Fortune*, March 28, 2024, https://fortune.com/2024/03/27/birkin-hermes-better-investment-than-gold/.

122 *her bag weighed as much as a dead donkey*: Crawford, *C'est Jane, Birkin Jane.*

122 *"Try bottling that to sell a product"*: Liana Satenstein, "What's 'Everyday Aspirational'—A Rant, a Rave!" *NEVERWORNS* (newsletter), July 20, 2023, https://neverworns.substack.com/p/whats-everyday-aspirationala-rant.

122 *for luxury goods to function as status symbols*: W. David Marx, *Status and Culture: How Our Desire for Social Rank Creates Taste, Identity, Art, Fashion, and Constant Change* (New York: Penguin, 2022).

123 *"coveted piece in the history of fashion"*: Tina Isaac-Goizé, "The Best-Kept Vintage Secret in Paris," *New York Times*, February 28, 2022, https://www.nytimes.com/2022/02/28/style/catherine-b-vintage-chanel-hermes.html.

123 *She spoke rarely about the agreement*: Rosemary Feitelberg, "Jane Birkin, Beyond the Bag," *WWD*, February 13, 2017, https://wwd.com/feature/jane-birkin-beyond-the-bag-5421382-761013/.

124 *Hermès paid a reported $40,000 annually*: Hannah Malach, "How Jane Birkin Helped Design Hermès' Most Popular Handbag: Her Inspiration, Royalties and What She Really Thinks About Its Namesake," *WWD*, July 17, 2023, https://wwd.com/pop-culture/culture-news/did-jane-birkin-design-the-birkin-bag-1235745565/.

124 *Christie's auction house set a world record*: "An Exceptional, Matte White Himalaya Niloticus Crocodile Diamond Birkin 30 with 18k White Gold & Diamond Hardware," https://www.christies.com/lot/lot-6000022.

125 *"I already have one"*: Crawford, *C'est Jane, Birkin Jane.*

CHAPTER FOURTEEN: AND YOU, ALWAYS

127 *Roger Ebert called it "the best film"*: Roger Ebert, "An Artist Reawakens Because of His Obnoxious Muse (1992)," posted April 12, 2009, https://www.rogerebert.com/reviews/la-belle-noiseuse-1991.

127 *"There were songs that he wrote for me when we were together"*: Jessica Hundley, "Musician/Actress Jane Birkin," Interviews with Icons (website), January 13, 2012, https://interviewswithicons.wordpress.com/2012/01/13/actressmusician-jane-birkin/.

128 *Serge was everything to me*: Robinson, "The Secret World of Serge Gainsbourg."

129 *"Jacques (Doillon) is not a violent man at all"*: Manceaux, "Entrez dans ma maison," *Marie Claire.*

130 *"We lay down beside him and time stopped"*: Kim Willsher, "'A Salon, a Studio, a Brothel': Inside Serge Gainsbourg's Paris Home," *Guardian*, October 5, 2023, https://www.theguardian.com/music/2023/oct/01/a-salon-a-studio-a-brothel-inside-serge-gainsbourgs-paris-home.

CHAPTER FIFTEEN: THE BAG IS GOING TO SING NOW

134 *claimed not to have known who Birkin was*: Georgina Brown, "Trojan Woman," *Independent*, March 15, 1995, https://www.the-independent.com/arts-entertainment/trojan-woman-1611307.html.

136 *guardian of the Gainsbourg-Birkin temple*: "Charlotte Gainsbourg, une star so french qui brille dans 'Étoile,'" Nedjma Van Egmond, *Le Parisien Week-End*, April 18, 2025, https://www.leparisien.fr/culture-loisirs/series/charlotte-gainsbourg-une-star-so-french-qui-brille-dans-etoile-la-serie-ma-occupee-pendant-neuf-mois-18-04-2025-JL3QIYHQ3REKNAX46EAELICG5I.php?ts=1744978591731.

136 *My mother has continued my father's work*: Marc-André Lussier, "Une mère, une fille et deux fantômes," *La Presse*, March 16, 2022, https://www.lapresse.ca/cinema/entrevues/2022-03-16/charlotte-gainsbourg-et-jane-par-charlotte/une-mere-une-fille-et-deux-fantomes.php.

136 *"When Jane Birkin floats on to the stage wearing a red dress"*: Solomons, "'Serge Needed All the Love.'"

136 *"If she finds herself . . . mourning the death of both Serge and her father"*: Liz Jobey, *New Statesman*, April, 11, 1997.

137 *"sort of delightful"*: "Jane, je t'aime toujours; Jane Birkin Barbican," *London Evening Standard,* March 3, 2003, link.gale.com/apps/doc/A98277442/OVIC?u=asuniv&sid=bookmark-OVIC&xid=7ea30fe2.

137 *Alain Delon, her costar from* La piscine: "French Legend Delon 'Supports' Far-Right," France 24, September 10, 2013, https://www.france24.com/en/20131009-french-actor-alain-delon-national-front.

138 *public statements*: "Brigitte Bardot on Trial for Muslim Slur," Reuters, April 15, 2008, https://www.reuters.com/article/lifestyle/brigitte-bardot-on-trial-for-muslim-slur-idUSL15847991/.

138 *Gérard Depardieu, who was found guilty*: Hugh Schofeld, "Gérard Depardieu Found Guilty in Sexual Assault Trial," BBC.com, May 13, 2025, https://www.bbc.com/news/articles/cg5v7ny40q2o.

138 *"it's what makes you feel good that counts"*: Rachel Halliburton, "Nous vous aimons," *New Statesman*, March 14, 2005.

140 *"She was lonely and unhappy when they met"*: Crawford, *C'est Jane, Birkin Jane.*

140 *"Jane walking on the beach"*: Crawford, *C'est Jane, Birkin Jane.*

CHAPTER SIXTEEN: AUTOFICTION

143 *Rolin offered another interpretation of the title*: Jane Birkin, *Boxes* (Paris: Avant Scène, 2021).

143 *Exarchopoulos . . . remembered going into one of Birkin's own bathrooms*: Louise Servans, "'Tu peux prendre un bain et manger du chocolat': Adèle Exarchopoulos raconte sa première visite chez Jane Birkin à 13 ans," *Madame Figaro*, August 24, 2023.

145 *"worrying, unpredictable, and touching sincerity"*: "'Boxes': Un auto portrait éparpillé," *Le Figaro*, June 6, 2007.

CHAPTER SEVENTEEN: AND YOU'RE AS PRETTY AS EVER

147 *"Patti Smith sort of stringy way"*: C. S., "Here's Looking at You," *Vogue*, July 2007.

147 *"It's the sort of age"*: Nechamkin, "Jane Birkin on Her Regrets."

147 *"Otherwise, it becomes terrifying"*: Alexa Chung, "What Jane Birkin and Her Style Meant to Me," *Financial Times*, July 21, 2023, https://www.ft.com/content/19cd3940-e7e6-4622-9343-555f0cb2b77c.

148 *She didn't like the look of a frown*: Crawford, *C'est Jane, Birkin Jane.*

148 *"And I said, 'My beauty'"*: Silva-Jelly, "Jane Birkin Opens Up About Her Ageless Style."

149 *"I try to tell myself I don't mind"*: Zoe Ruffner, "Jane Birkin on Her New Album and the Only Three Makeup Products She Uses at 74," *Vogue*, January 22, 2021, https://www.vogue.com/article/jane-birkin-interview-oh-pardon-tu-dormais.

149 *"She made me food"*: *Elle* [France], December 11, 2020.

151 *"At first, I was better known because of my family"*: Kim Willsher, "Jane Birkin's Daughter Kate Barry Dies After Fall from Paris Flat," *Guardian*, December 12, 2013, https://www.theguardian.com/world/2013/dec/12/jane-birkin-daughter-kate-barry-dies-fall-paris-flat.

151 *"Initially surrounded by the images of others"*: *Kate Barry: My Own Space* (Éditions de la Martinière, 2023).

152 *"I spent my time under the tables"*: Sylvain Menétrey, "Lou Doillon, artiste protéiforme: 'J'aime être une Shiva à plusieurs bras,'" *T: Le magazine du Temps*, December 16, 2023.

152 *She started ditching school regularly at fourteen*: Nechamkin, "Jane Birkin on Her Regrets."

152 *"She got the part and I said, 'Go for it'"*: Nechamkin, "Jane Birkin on Her Regrets."

153 *"Neither daughter feels she has her mother's beauty"*: Sarah Mower, "Skinny Genes," *Vogue*, April 2009, https://archive.vogue.com/article/2009/04/01/skinny-genes.

154 *"I wanted it to smell like"*: "How We Met: Jane Birkin and Lyn Harris," *Independent*, September 18, 2010, https://www.the-independent.com/news/people/profiles/how-we-met-jane-birkin-amp-lyn-harris-2080200.html.

CHAPTER EIGHTEEN: AFRAID OF SOLITUDE

155 *consulted two "shrinks"—her term*: Birkin, *Post-Scriptum.*

156 *"She started drinking a little again, from time to time"*: "Kate Barry :

pour son fils Roman, sa mort n'était pas accidentelle," *Paris Match*, October 19, 2023, https://www.parismatch.com/people/kate-barry-pour-son-fils-roman-sa-mort-netait-pas-accidentelle-230688.

157 *antidepressants . . . his mother was taking for depression*: "Kate Barry: Pour son fils Roman, sa mort n'était pas accidentelle," *Paris Match*, October 19, 2023,

159 *One regular visitor to the cemetery*: "Au Revoir, Jane Birkin," *France with Véro* (blog), August 2, 2023, https://francewithvero.com/blog/au-revoir-jane-birkin/.

CHAPTER NINETEEN: SPECTERS

160 *"the most important thing that had happened to me"*: A. D. Amorisi, "Loss, Love, and Lust: In Conversation with Jane Birkin," *Flood*, March 9, 2021, https://floodmagazine.com/85538/in-conversation-jane-birkin-oh-pardon-tu-dormais/.

160 *"I was listening to an old program on the radio yesterday"*: Ruffner, "Jane Birkin on Her New Album."

160 *she focused on anecdotes "that make things real"*: Ruffner, "Jane Birkin on Her New Album."

161 *"suffused with the darkly tinted wisdom of a life entering its winter"*: Jeff Weiss, "Jane Birkin Is Back with a New Album, but Her Presence Is Everlasting," *Washington Post*, March 18, 2021, https://www.washingtonpost.com/entertainment/music/jane-birkin-interview-album/2021/03/17/6bf2b336-8676-11eb-bfdf-4d36dab83a6d_story.html.

161 Pitchfork *compared it to late-period masterpieces*: Ben Cardew, "Jane Birkin: Oh! Pardon tu dormais . . . ," *Pitchfork*, February 17, 2021, https://pitchfork.com/reviews/albums/jane-birkin-oh-pardon-tu-dormais/.

162 *"I would love to make a line of my own"*: Ruffner, "Jane Birkin on Her New Album."

162 *I wanted to stop. . . . I didn't like the questions*: Michael Odmark, "The Close-Up: Jane Birkin and Charlotte Gainsbourg," *Filmlinc Daily*, February 3, 2016, https://www.filmlinc.org/daily/the-close-up-jane-birkin-and-charlotte-gainsbourg/.

163 *She "might have made the film for no one but herself"*: Beatrice Loayza, "'Jane by Charlotte' Review: A Mother-Daughter Duet," *New York Times*, March 17, 2022, https://www.nytimes.com/2022/03/17/movies/jane-by-charlotte-review.html.

163 *A* Variety *review called it "sloppy"*: Peter Debruge, "'Jane by Charlotte' Review: Jane Birkin's Daughter Doodles a Hazy Sketch of Her

Famous Mom," *Variety*, February 27, 2023, https://variety.com/2021/film/reviews/jane-by-charlotte-review-jane-birkin-1235011349/.

CHAPTER TWENTY: YOUR JANE B.

166 *"Jane had been unwell for a long time"*: Charlotte Rampling, "Jane Birkin Remembered by Charlotte Rampling," *Guardian*, December 18, 2023, https://www.theguardian.com/culture/2023/dec/17/obituaries-2023-jane-birkin-remembered-by-charlotte-rampling.

167 *"Before, when I was asked how I wanted to die"*: Ellen Burney, "Jane Birkin, Musician, Actor, and Style Icon, Has Died at 76," *Vogue*, July 16, 2023, https://www.vogue.com/article/jane-birkin-obituary.

167 *held her hand while she was in the hospital*: Crawford, *C'est Jane, Birkin Jane.*

167 *"She had decided it"*: Peter Allen, "Jane Birkin Died 'On Her First Night Alone for Almost Two Years,' Family Reveal," *Standard* (London), July 19, 2023, https://www.standard.co.uk/news/world/jane-birkin-died-paris-first-night-alone-two-years-family-statement-b1095317.html.

168 *"come to pay tribute to our little Englishwoman"*: Robert Greenall, "Jane Birkin Paris Funeral Draws Celebrities and Crowds," *BBC News*, July 24, 2023, https://www.bbc.co.uk/news/entertainment-arts-66294457.

169 *"Until I was about thirty, I wasn't required"*: Laura Barnett, "Portrait of the Artist: Jane Birkin, Singer and Actor," *Guardian*, November 25, 2017, https://www.theguardian.com/film/2008/jan/22/popandrock.

169 *"Singer, Actress, Fashion Inspiration"*: Constant Méheut and Alex Traub, "Jane Birkin, Singer, Actress and Fashion Inspiration, Dies at 76," *New York Times*, July 16, 2023, https://www.nytimes.com/2023/07/16/arts/music/jane-birkin-dead.html.

169 *She sings "Jane B." alongside Franco-Belgian cellist Camille Thomas*: "Camille Thomas, Jane Birkin, Julien Brocal—Jane B (Feat. Jane Birkin)," posted June 9, 2023, by Deutsche Grammophon, YouTube, https://www.youtube.com/watch?v=WmE6kMWkQpA.

EPILOGUE

172 *"a little Jane Birkin, a little New England summer ease"*: Gwyneth Paltrow, "We made @goop's new color blur balms," September 16, 2023, Instagram, https://www.instagram.com/gwynethpaltrow/reel/CxQm3n7uHFI/?hl=en.

174 *France is "usually about ten years behind England"*: Oscar Holland, "Birkin on Serge Gainsbourg, #MeToo and That Handbag," CNN, February 21, 2020, https://www.cnn.com/style/article/jane-birkin-serge-gainsbourg/index.html.

174 *"I know for a fact that Deneuve is a feminist"*: Lisa Armstrong, "Jane Birkin Interview: 'Why Didn't I Think My Work Was Interesting?'" *Telegraph*, July 16, 2023, https://www.telegraph.co.uk/fashion/people/jane-birkin-interview-actor-singer-hermes-bag-moi-non-plus/.

175 *"I don't think it equated with the Serge that any of us knew"*: Potton, "Jane Birkin on the Truth."

INDEX

Note: JB *refers to Jane Birkin, and* SG *refers to Serge Gainsbourg.*

G

ABOUT THE AUTHOR

Marisa Meltzer is a journalist based in New York who, for over two decades, has covered the beauty, fashion, wellness, and celebrity industries for top national publications such as *The New York Times*, *The New Yorker*, *The Guardian*, *The Wall Street Journal*, *Vogue*, and *Vanity Fair*. She is the author of the *New York Times* bestseller *Glossy*, *This Is Big*, and *Girl Power*, and the coauthor of *How* Sassy *Changed My Life*.

Atria Books, an imprint of Simon & Schuster, fosters an open environment where ideas flourish, bestselling authors soar to new heights, and tomorrow's finest voices are discovered and nurtured. Since its launch in 2002, Atria has published hundreds of bestsellers and extraordinary books, which would not have been possible without the invaluable support and expertise of its team and publishing partners. Thank you to the Atria Books colleagues who collaborated on *It Girl* as well as to the hundreds of professionals in the Simon & Schuster advertising, audio, communications, design, ebook, finance, human resources, legal, marketing, operations, production, sales, supply chain, subsidiary rights, and warehouse departments who help Atria bring great books to light.

EDITORIAL
Kate Napolitano
Hannah Frankel

JACKET DESIGN
Emma A. Van Deum

MARKETING
Zakiya Jamal
Morgan Pager

MANAGING EDITORIAL
Paige Lytle
Shelby Pumphrey
Sofia Echeverry

PRODUCTION
Nancy Tonik
Brigid Black
Joal Hetherington
Davina Mock-Maniscalco

PUBLICITY
Falon Kirby
Debbie Norflus
Molly Burgoyne

PUBLISHING OFFICE
Suzanne Donahue
Abby Velasco

SUBSIDIARY RIGHTS
Nicole Bond
Sara Bowne
Rebecca Justiniano
Germanie Louis